what MUSICAL INSTRUMENT for me?

By JACK LEVINE
and TAKERU IIJIMA

Illustrated by S. MATSUDA

BAILEY BROS & SWINFEN LTD

FOLKESTONE

S.B.N. 561 00072 7
Published by Bailey Bros & Swinfen Ltd.
Folkestone

Printed in Great Britain by
Stephen Austin and Sons Ltd., Hertford

Contents

To Sheri, Lynne and Chris

ACKNOWLEDGMENTS

For the photographs used in this book, the authors wish to thank: The Baldwin Piano Co., Cincinnati, Ohio, 26, 29; C. G. Conn, Ltd., Elkhart, Indiana, 56, 57, 60, 62, 63, 65, 69, 70, 76, 77, 79, 80, 81, 84, 86, 87, 88; Goya Guitars, New York, 50; International Accordion Manufacturing Co., East Detroit, Michigan, 105; Kay Musical Instrument Co., Chicago, Illinois, 43, 44; Lyon and Healy, New York, 48; Roth Violins, Cleveland, Ohio, 38, 46; Slingerland Drum Co., Chicago, Illinois, 98; Steinway and Sons, New York, 23, 30. Thanks also to Eleanor Morrison of Columbia Records, New York.

1. HOW DO I GET STARTED?

As you read this book and look at the pictures of the large variety of instruments of all sizes and shapes, you will realize that surely there is one for you! Playing an instrument or singing is a wonderful way to express yourself — your joy, your gaiety, tenderness and even sadness. Besides being a creative art, playing music is a lot of fun. It gives you a feeling of satisfaction and accomplishment, and it also gives you the perfect answer to that well-known question, "What can I do now?"

Music does something else for you. It helps your physical development. To play correctly you have to sit and stand correctly — head up and shoulders back. You can't slouch and perform properly, so you naturally develop good posture. If you play a blowing instrument or sing, you will develop strong lung power, and if you play a fingering instrument, your fingers will become more nimble. Playing music will train you to listen closely and use your ears keenly.

Am I Musical?

If you like to sing or whistle or listen to music, you are musical!

People sometimes think that being musical means being especially gifted, but that is far from true. It would be a pretty sad world if none of us attempted to do anything unless we knew we were geniuses at it! If you can learn to read and write, you can learn to read music and play a musical instrument.

A physical handicap need not prevent you from enjoying the pleasure of music. In fact, music is an especially good hobby for the handicapped person whose other activities may be limited. If you have a physical handicap of almost any sort except deafness you can learn to play certain instruments. For instance, you need your hands for any instrument except voice (the voice is certainly a very versatile instrument), but you can learn to play a great many instruments without the use of your legs. Blindness is not really a handicap to musicians, although they must learn to play without reading the actual music.

We know a partially blind boy who learned to play the clarinet. Since he could hardly see, he had to sit very close to the music stand before him. But he developed a good memory, and after several readings, was able to play most of the music from memory. This young man became one of the outstanding student clarinetists of his town.

If you have protruding teeth and want to play a blowing instrument, it is a good idea to get your dentist's advice first.

What Musical Team?

One of the most wonderful things about playing a musical instrument is playing with a group. It's like playing on a winning football team where each member must do his job well and in time with everyone else. There are many different kinds of musical groups, and if you know the kind you would like to play with, it may help you make up your mind when it comes to choosing the right musical instrument for you.

What kinds of musical groups are there? A band, orchestra, dance band, marching band? A small string, woodwind, brass or percussion "ensemble" (group)? A vocal ensemble? If you have a preference, keep it in mind when selecting your instrument. For instance, you can play in a band or a marching band if you select an instrument of the woodwind, brass or percussion families, but not a string instrument. But in an orchestra the strings are the most important instruments!

If you enjoy performing alone you can, of course, give solo performances on any instrument. However, if you think you would like to be a concert performer in the classical field, the piano, violin and voice are most often featured.

What About a Teacher?

In order to learn to play, you need a teacher. In most large cities and metropolitan areas you'll find qualified instructors for every instrument. Before you make a definite choice, make sure that a teacher of the particular instrument you choose is available in your area.

Many public and private schools now teach instruments as a regular course and usually instruments are provided along with the instruction. Check to see if your school offers such classes. This is a wonderful opportunity to get some early training and to see whether you like the instrument of your choice. Many fine musicians started in such a program. You will also gain valuable group experience. The only limitation of this program is that the number of students in the class usually prevents individual instruction, even where necessary. Therefore you should start private instruction along with the class instruction if you can. Both types of training are valuable for the beginning student.

Big or Little?

In choosing a musical instrument you must consider your own physical size and the size of the instrument. As you will see, some instruments come in different sizes so that there is no problem at all. Some instruments are so small that even the smallest child can handle them, while the piano is so big that your size doesn't matter.

If you decide that you want to play an instrument that's too big for you now – the baritone saxophone, for example – you can begin on one of the smaller related instruments. What you learn on one instrument you can always apply to the instrument of your choice when you grow big enough to handle it.

Another thing to consider about the size of your instrument is how you are going to get it from place to place. Again, the very small instrument presents no problem, and the piano stays put. You are not expected to bring your own piano but the drummer has to carry his drums. And the big bass fiddle – the double bass – has to be transported too. This may or may not be a problem for you, but it is something to think about before you choose a very large instrument: how you will get it from place to place.

Before Buying

Don't rush to your music store to make a purchase as soon as you've decided. A much better idea is to take a few months as a try-out period to see if your choice was a good one. Most music stores will rent you an instrument monthly for a reasonable fee. Some stores even offer a rental-purchase plan – they allow you to subtract the rental cost from the purchase price when you're ready to buy a new instrument. You can ask your neighborhood music store owner if he has this rental-purchase plan.

If you make progress within the first few months and you are pleased with your choice, then you are ready to purchase. If possible, ask your teacher or someone who plays the instrument well to try it out before you buy it. *Try before you buy.* You can't judge by the looks of a shiny new instrument and a plush velvet case. An instrument must be well regulated and must play in tune. Only a musician or a qualified teacher can properly check these requirements.

All manufacturers produce instruments to sell at different prices. Some of the less expensive instruments are called student models and are adequate for beginning students. The more expensive models are professional instruments. During the first few years, you can use the student model. As you become more proficient, you'll want to buy a professional model. A good professional instrument can last a lifetime with proper care, but don't buy an expensive model unless you are absolutely certain that you will continue to play.

There's also the possibility of buying a second-hand instrument. Here again, have your teacher or a qualified player try out the instrument. Remember, the two important things to keep in mind are: "Is it in good working order?" And, "Does it play in tune?" In the case of a wooden instrument, examine it carefully to see if there are any cracks. A cracked instrument cannot be properly repaired and is of little worth regardless of the price.

When buying an instrument with a mouthpiece, it's

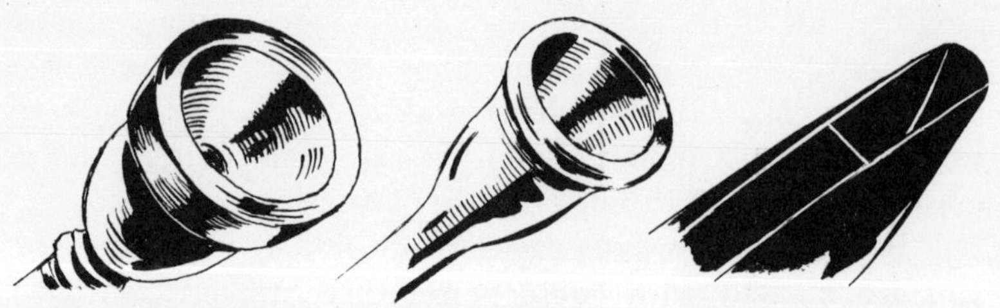

1. There are different kinds of mouthpieces for brass and woodwind instruments. From left to right are the mouthpieces for trumpet, French horn and clarinet.

quite possible that the mouthpiece will not fit your needs. Mouthpieces come in standard sizes and you may require a special mouthpiece. You should ask your teacher to help you find the right mouthpiece for you, and buy it at the same time you purchase your instrument.

And just to remind you once again, check to see whether your school has a musical program which includes the loan of the instrument you are learning to play. Then you can postpone buying your own instrument for a while, and when the time does come, you'll know exactly what you want.

What Is My Future in Music?

The demand for musicians is growing constantly, and the study of music may lead you to a profitable vocation in life. Learning to play an instrument may be the "Open Sesame" for a musical future for you in any one, or all, of the following fields:

First, if you are an exceptional musician, the concert field is open to you, where you perform as a soloist. This is a most difficult area of musical activity and requires the highest degree of ability.

Second, you can become a member of a professional

group (orchestra, band, ensemble) if you are extremely proficient on your instrument.

Third, you can train to teach music privately or in a private or public school, in which case you must not only be able to play your instrument well but you must be able to teach it too. School teaching requires a college degree but this isn't necessary if you decide to give private lessons.

Fourth, you can work at another job and play music on a part-time basis in the evenings and on weekends. Very often, orchestra and band musicians are also employed in work completely out of the music field.

Finally, and very important, if you don't want to be a professional musician you can play an instrument purely for enjoyment and relaxation, alone or with a group. Another nice thing about playing an instrument is that performances by other musicians will give you greater pleasure, especially when the performer happens to be playing the instrument you play.

Music adds to everyone's life. Not a day goes by that you do not hear some kind of music. But the best way to enjoy music is to participate.

Suggested Recordings

As you have seen, there are many things to think about in choosing an instrument, but so far we haven't mentioned one of the most important – its sound! You have to like the music your instrument makes! The best way to find out about that is to listen to an expert playing the instrument you have in mind, and in order to help you, we have added a list of "Suggested Recordings" of the instruments discussed in this book. Go to your library, if it has recordings, or to your music store, and listen to as many of them as you can. Listen particularly for the instrument you want to hear, and play each record as often as you care to. Don't expect to play your instrument that well, of course, but realize that that is how it can sound when played by a fine performer. Perhaps in time you may be able to reach that high level too!

2. THE PIANO and ORGAN

Piano

Of all the musical instruments, the piano is the most popular, and no wonder. It is one of the few instruments with which you can produce full, complete music without the help of any other instruments. You can play any type of music on the piano from classical to all kinds of jazz.

The piano is a basic instrument in any dance band, but all by itself it can produce such melody, harmony and rhythm that people can dance to its music. At informal gatherings and parties, wherever there is a piano and a piano player, the pianist is usually the center of attention and activity as people gather round to sing popular songs and old favorites. No wonder the piano is the most popular musical instrument!

The piano is used to accompany singers or instrumentalists. It plays an important role in the school orchestra, although it is not used in a symphony orchestra except as a solo instrument.

The piano is a string instrument, because vibrating strings produce the sound. It is also a percussion instrument, because a striking action sets the strings into motion.

There are two types of pianos, grand and upright, and they come in many sizes. Naturally, the finer the instrument the better the tone, but any piano that can be kept in tune is satisfactory for a beginner to learn on.

Have you ever looked inside a piano? If you have, then you know it's like a complicated piece of machinery, much like the motor under the hood of an automobile. Like the automobile engine, the piano is made up of hundreds of parts. In the upright piano there are over 40 parts for each key! In the grand piano, there are over 70 parts for each key! Multiply each of these parts by 88 – the number of keys in a standard piano – and you get an idea of the total number of parts. If any one part is broken or not working properly, it can cause the key not to play.

When you press the piano keys, you set this machinery in motion. Small wooden hammers covered with hard felt strike the strings and cause them to vibrate. The hammers allow you to produce tones ranging from loud to soft, depending on the force you use to press the keys. (The name piano is short for "pianoforte," which in Italian means "soft-loud.")

The shiny metal pedals which you work with your feet also affect the sound. The one on the right controls the dampers. The damper is a device which touches the string as soon as you release the key, and so stops the vibration. Without the damper, the string would continue to vibrate even while you played other notes, and you would get a jumbled sound. However, sometimes you *want* the notes to continue vibrating and when you step on the damper pedal, that is what happens: all the dampers move away from the strings and the strings vibrate freely, even after you take your fingers off the keys.

The left pedal is the soft pedal. It makes the piano sound softer. On some pianos there is a middle pedal, called the *sostenuto* pedal. When you play notes and then press this pedal, those notes that you just played will

2. This grand piano is a complicated and magnificent instrument. Any piano, if it is kept in tune, is satisfactory for you to learn on.

continue to sound. Few musical compositions require this pedal and many pianos do not have it at all.

If you have a piano, open the top and look at the strings. There are over 200 of them. Try plucking a few and see what happens. You will notice that the heavier strings produce a low sound and the thinner strings produce higher sounds. The pitch (the level of sound, high or low) of the string depends on three things: the length, thickness (or weight) and tightness of the string.

Notice the way the strings are arranged. You will find that if you touch a key at the right side of the keyboard, the hammer will strike a group of three strings. In the middle of the keyboard the hammer strikes two strings. At the left a single thick wire sounds the notes. That is because it takes three fine strings to produce a rich full sound for the high notes; it takes two of the heavier strings for the middle notes to produce an equally rich sound; and one of the very heavy strings does the same job for the low notes.

The richness of sound of a piano is also increased by the soundboard, which is under the strings in a grand piano and behind the strings in an upright. When you press a key, not only the strings vibrate, but the soundboard as well, and the air between the soundboard and strings vibrates too. The total vibration of strings, soundboard and air produces the rich tone of the piano.

Part of a keyboard is pictured in Illus. 3. Notice the white and black keys. The black keys are arranged in alternate groups of two's and three's. They produce notes which sound in between the sounds made by the white keys on either side.

Each key on the keyboard has a letter name. In music, we use only the first 7 letters of the alphabet. Starting with the key marked "A," each white key that follows uses the next letter of the alphabet. After "G," the letters repeat. One way to learn the location of notes on the keyboard is to remember that the letter "C" is always just to the left of the double black keys, and "F" is always just to the left of the three black keys. Therefore, whenever you see two black keys, you know that the white key to the left is "C," and each time you see three black keys, the white key to the left is "F."

Piano music is written on two staffs. Each staff is made up of five lines and four spaces, and has a *clef* (meaning key in French) sign. You add lines (called ledger lines) above and below a staff for additional notes.

3. Each key of the piano is called by a letter name, from A to G. The notes in the bass and treble clefs match the keys on the keyboard.

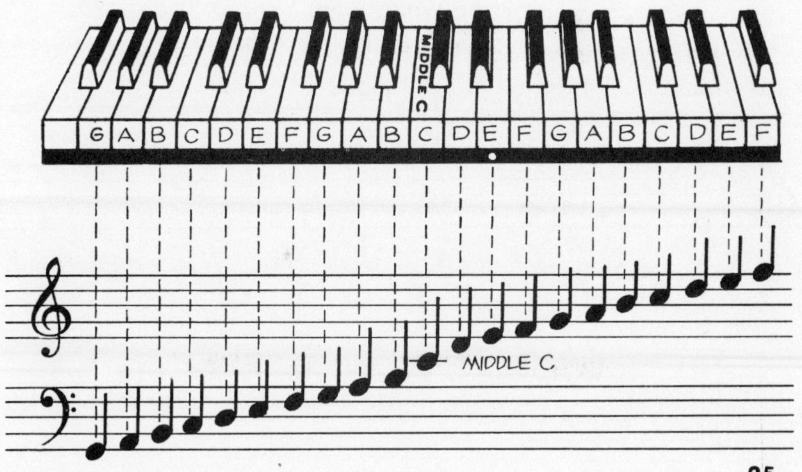

4. Notice how the black keys are arranged in alternate groups of two's and three's. Their sound is in between the sound of the white keys.

The treble clef, also called the "G" clef, which is used for the higher-pitched notes, looks like this:

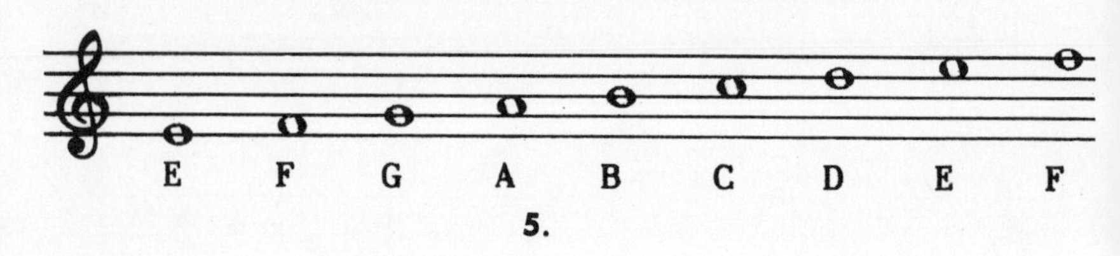

5.

You see that the bottom line is "E" and the space just above is "F." The five lines, then, are E-G-B-D-F, and the spaces, F-A-C-E.

The bass clef or "F" clef is used for the lower-pitched notes and it looks like this:

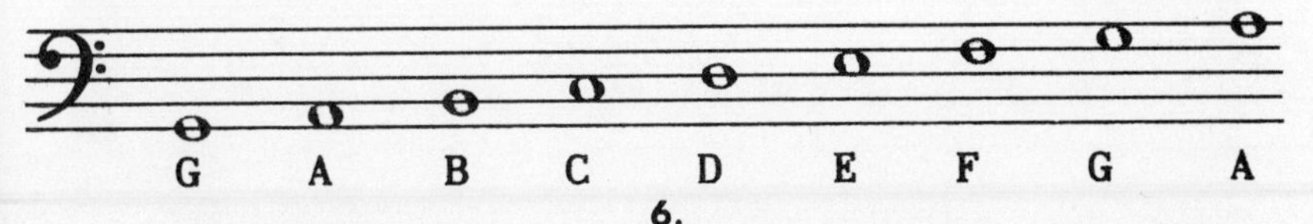

6.

In this clef, the note on the bottom line is a low "G." The space just above is "A." The five lines on the bass clef, then, are G-B-D-F-A, and the spaces, A-C-E-G.

You use both of these clefs when you play the piano. Usually, the right hand plays the treble clef and the left hand plays the bass clef.

By picturing the keyboard and the clefs together, we show how the notes in the clefs match the keys on the keyboard. (Middle C is on a ledger line between the two clefs!) See Illustration 3 on page 25.

Now, let's try to play a piece on the piano. You're probably familiar with the song, "Merrily We Roll Along." It's written this way in the treble clef:

7.

Try to play this using your right hand. Start with the B which is just above middle C. (The wiggly line is just a rest, or pause.)

Here is the same melody in the bass clef:

8.

Try to play this using your left hand. It also starts on B. You can find it from Illus. 8. The difference in sound is very obvious, as you can hear.

You can try this with both hands at the same time (as below). It will be difficult at first but learning to play the piano with both hands comes with practice.

9.

10. Playing the piano will give you great pleasure, and you can entertain your family and friends too. You will also find that your knowledge will help you to enjoy all other music.

When you play more than one note at the same time, it is called a chord. And this is what the piano student faces – learning to read and play many notes at the same time.

We have found, in teaching music, that most students who already know how to play the piano can learn to play other instruments more easily than other beginners. Learning to play the piano even slightly helps you become a better musician and increases your enjoyment of music. Listen to a few of the following recordings of piano music.

11. The piano owes its beginnings to the simple string instruments of ancient Greece and Asia. The lyre, the psaltery, the dulcimer, and the harpsichord and clavichord all contributed to the piano's development. Even the names of those lovely instruments of old sound like music!

In the clavichord, pictured above, a piece of metal called a tangent strikes the string to produce a sound. In the harpsichord, below, a quill plucks the string when a key is pressed. In the beginning of the 18th century, Bartolomeo Cristofori, an Italian harpsichord maker, put hammers on his instrument instead of quills or tangents. The piano was born.

Suggested Recordings

Any of the Beethoven *Sonatas* (such as *The Moonlight Sonata, Op. 27, No. 2*)
Debussy: *Children's Corner*
Gershwin: *Rhapsody in Blue*
Handel: *Harmonious Blacksmith*
Liszt: *Dance of the Gnomes*
Liszt: *Hungarian Rhapsody* (any of the several Rhapsodies)
Saint-Saëns: *Carnival of the Animals*

Organ

Most majestic of musical instruments is the pipe organ, an instrument of tremendous size and sound. It's hard to believe, but this huge instrument developed from the tiny pipes of Pan which were hollow reeds tied together, held in the hand and played by blowing.

Early organs were cumbersome instruments that needed several men to pump air into the bellows. A bellow is like the lung in the human body – it holds air. This air in the bellows creates air columns in the pipes which produce the sound. With the coming of electricity, motors replaced this manpower.

The modern pipe organ consists of two or more keyboards (called manuals), a pedal board (another keyboard played with the feet) and the pipes. The number of pipes depends on the size of the organ. A large organ has as many as 2,500 pipes! If you have a chance to visit the pipe room of a building which houses a pipe organ, you'll find it fascinating. Actually, the pipes that you see in a church, or wherever there is an organ, are only decorative pipes, and the real pipes are hidden behind these in what is called the pipe room. Here you will see rows and rows of pipes, a different set of pipes for each stop (or lever). There are a number of these stops or levers on the organ, and each one produces a different kind of sound when it is pressed.

Today there are many kinds of electronic organs which are ideal for the home because they're much smaller, have no pipes, and are, of course, far less expensive. You play the electronic organ in much the same way as the pipe organ. There is one or more manual, a pedal board and stops. Electromagnetic waves which are amplified produce the tone. There is also a small electronic organ with buttons at the left of the keyboard. These buttons resemble the buttons on the accordion – each one plays a complete chord. You press them with your left hand while you play the melody with your right hand.

To play the organ, you must first learn to play the piano. A big problem for the pipe organ student is simply trying to find an organ to practice on. It's usually hard to find a good organ teacher too. This isn't the case with the electronic organ, however. You'll have no difficulty playing it if you know how to play the piano.

3. THE STRINGS

Have you ever noticed how much the string instruments resemble a real family? The violin, viola, violoncello and double bass look like brothers and sisters. Except for size, the four instruments are quite similar – each has four strings and each is played with a bow. The violin is the smallest and sounds the highest; the double bass is largest and sounds the lowest. They are often referred to as "the violin family."

One of the best things about learning to play any of the string instruments is that all four are made in various sizes to fit your individual needs. For instance, the violin is obtainable in three sizes – half size, three-quarter size and full size. This means that you can start with the size most comfortable to you. If you're young and small, you start on the half-size instrument, and as you grow, you move on to the three-quarter size and finally, the full size.

The earliest string instrument was probably discovered thousands of years ago when a prehistoric hunter pulled the bow-string of his hunting bow and found that it made a sound. The first string instruments used in ancient times were the lute and the lyre. The lute was used to accompany singing and storytelling and was originally plucked, but later it became a bowing instrument.

By the time of the Middle Ages, a whole family of strings named the fiedels had made its appearance – our word "fiddle" comes from its name. After the fiedels came

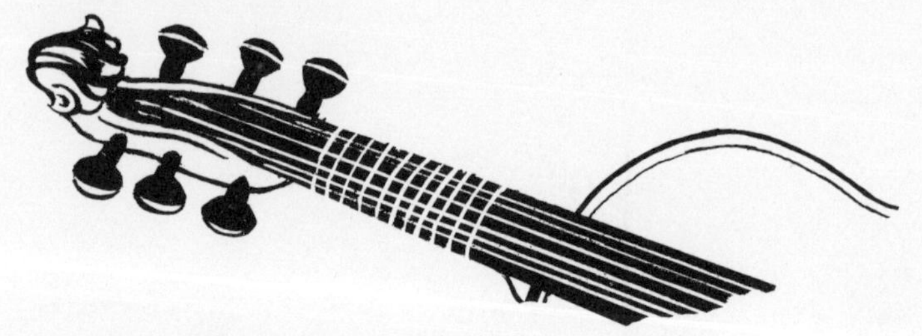

12. Frets, ridges on the fingerboard of old viols, guided the players in finding notes. Guitars still have frets today.

the viol family, which resembled our modern strings. These viols were six-stringed instruments with ridges called "frets" on the fingerboard (see Illus. 12). The viols were played while resting on or between the player's legs with the fingerboard upward.

The most famous violins in all the world today were made in the town of Cremona, Italy, during the 17th and 18th centuries. The Amati family, father and sons, were among the first craftsmen of the times to master the art of violin making. But their pupils, Guarnerius and Stradivarius, became even more famous violin makers.

Antonius Stradivarius achieved the greatest fame of all violin makers of Cremona. During his lifetime, he made over a thousand string instruments, mostly violins. The work was all done by hand, of course. About half of the instruments he made are still in existence today. Some of our leading violinists today own and perform on these same instruments made over 200 years ago. The genuine Stradivarius violins which originally sold for just a few dollars are now worth as much as $75,000! The reason for their great value is because they were perfectly made to produce the finest possible tone.

You often hear the string instruments compared to human voices. The violin represents the soprano voice, the viola the alto, the violoncello (commonly called just 'cello), the tenor, and the double bass is the bass voice.

The strings on these instruments are made of gut, fine wire, or gut wound with wire. Attached to a tailpiece, they stretch across a bridge over the length of the fingerboard to the peg box where they are wound around tuning pegs. You turn the pegs to tune each string: you tighten the string to make the pitch higher or loosen the string to lower the pitch. Also, the heavier strings are low-pitched while the lighter strings are high-pitched.

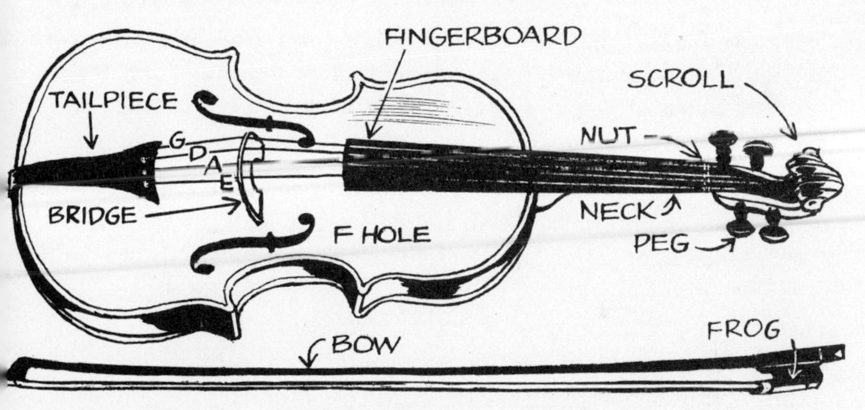

13. The strings are made of gut or wire attached to the tailpiece. From the fingerboard the strings stretch over a bridge to a peg box. Here they are wound around tuning pegs.

To produce a sound on a string instrument, you draw a bow across one of the strings. The bow was originally shaped like a hunter's bow and that's how it got its name. But unlike the hunter's bow, it curves slightly outward, rather than forward (or inward), as you can see in Illus. 14. Notice the strands of horse tail hair stretched from end to end. Before playing, you tighten the hairs by turning a screw at one end of the bow – the end that you hold –

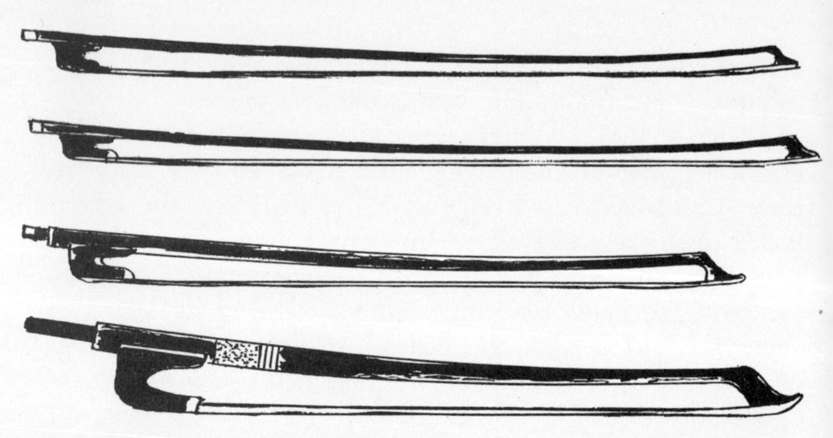

14. The bow has hair from a horse's tail stretched across it. This hair grips the strings, making them vibrate. From top to bottom, the bows are for violin, viola, cello and bass.

called the frog end. Draw the bow across a string. If you're unable to make a sound, perhaps you need to rub rosin on the hair of the bow. Rosin helps the hair to grip the strings. This grip or friction causes the strings to vibrate and produces the sound. The hollow body of the instrument reinforces the sound and makes it louder.

Here is an interesting experiment which will help you understand how vibration produces sound:

Stretch a rubber band around an open cigar box or a similar box. Pluck the rubber band and notice its rapid movement up and down as it vibrates and makes a sound. Tighten the rubber band and you'll find that as it moves even more rapidly, the sound becomes higher in pitch. Now use a heavier rubber band and you will get a lower sound.

The rubber band is like the string of the instrument and the box is its body or sound box. As you see, the pitch of the string depends on its tightness and also its weight or thickness. Length, too, is an important factor.

The four members of the violin family use similar

bows, but the larger the instrument, the shorter and heavier is the bow. There are two basic bowing strokes: up-bow and down-bow. The symbol for up-bow is (V) and for down-bow (⊓), in a musical piece; and the term for using the bow is arco. For up-bow, you start the bow at the tip and draw up to the frog. For down-bow, you reverse the direction. Always draw the bow in a parallel line between the bridge and the end of the fingerboard (see Illus. 18 on page 40).

Proper bowing controls all of the basic musical qualities: tone, expression and volume. The use of the bow plays such an important part in a string performance that two accomplished musicians, playing on the same instrument, can produce entirely different results. The more highly skilled the bowing, the finer will be the performance.

15. You can vary the sound of a stringed instrument by placing a mute over the bridge. These are some types of mutes.

You can produce many special effects on the string instruments. To get a muffled sound, place a mute over the bridge (see the illustration of mutes). By bowing across two strings at one time, you can play two notes together. Plucking the strings, called pizzicato, creates additional effects.

Now let's take a closer look at each of the four string instruments.

16. The viola (left) is almost a twin of the violin (right), except that it is larger and has longer and thicker strings.

Violin

The violin, which is the smallest of the group, is the highest-sounding. Look at the picture carefully and you will see the correct way to hold it. You play with the fingers of the left hand and bow with the right. It makes no difference whether you're right-handed or left-handed – you play the violin this way only!

The strings of the violin must be tuned to these notes:

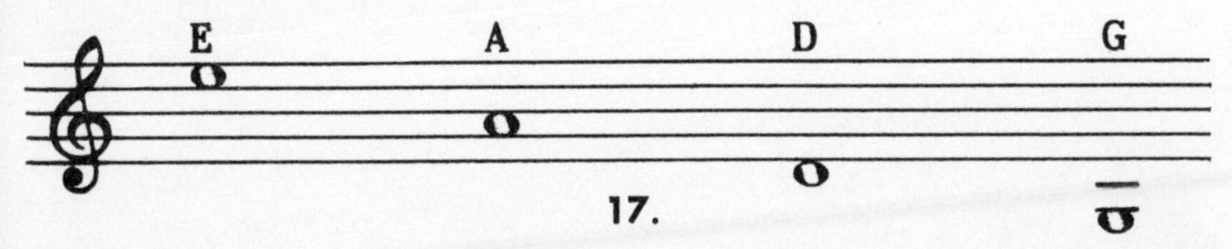

You can change the pitch of any string so that it will play a higher note. Place the first finger (the thumb is not used for fingering) on the string you're bowing and press firmly against the fingerboard. You get a higher sound because you've shortened the portion of the string which vibrates.

There are 30 or more violins in a large orchestra – the largest single group of instruments in the symphony orchestra. The violinist seated just to the left of the conductor is the concertmaster, leader of the entire string section.

The violin is used in all string ensembles (groups of various string instruments), in large dance orchestras, and, of course, quite frequently as a solo instrument.

Suggested Recordings

Kreisler: *Caprice Viennoise* and *Tamborin Chinois*
Handel: Overture to *The Messiah*
Massenet: *Meditation (Thais)*
Paganini: *Moto Perpetuo*
Sarasate: *Romanza Andaluza*

18. Positions for playing string instruments

Viola

The viola is the least known among the four string instruments. There's so little difference between the violin and viola that they look like twins, and unless you know them well, only by seeing them together can you tell one from the other. The viola is just a few inches larger than the violin. It is held and played the same way but the strings are longer and thicker and therefore sound a little lower than the violin.

You tune the strings of the viola to the following notes:

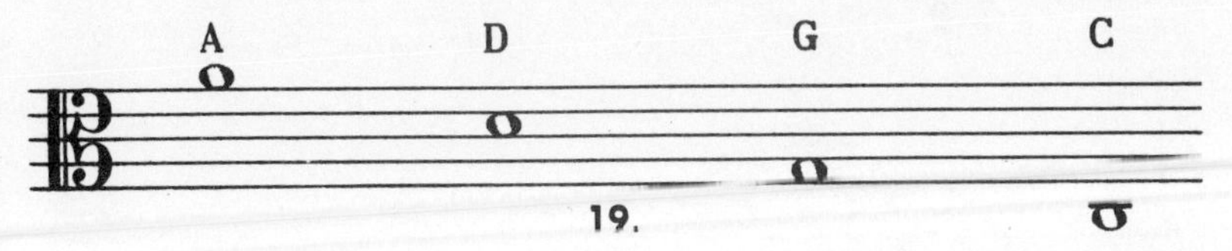

19.

Notice that viola music is written in a special clef, called viola clef or C clef. Middle C is located on the middle line.

The viola, too, is an orchestral instrument. You'll find 10 to 12 of them in a full symphonic orchestra and many string groups make important use of the viola.

SUGGESTED RECORDINGS

Debussy: *Trio for Flute, Viola and Harp*
Mendelssohn: *Hebrides Overture*
Mozart: *Sinfonia Concertante*

Cello

You've probably noticed the cellist (cello player) in an orchestra – he sits with the cello placed between his knees, the fingerboard extended over the left shoulder and the tailpin resting on the floor. If the cellist wants to check himself for correct position, he makes sure the peg box is about even with his left ear, and moves the tailpiece up or down to get this proper position. Then, like the violinist and violist, he bows with the right hand and fingers with the left. Since the cello is considerably larger than the violin and viola, the fingering differs.

The cello strings are tuned to these notes:

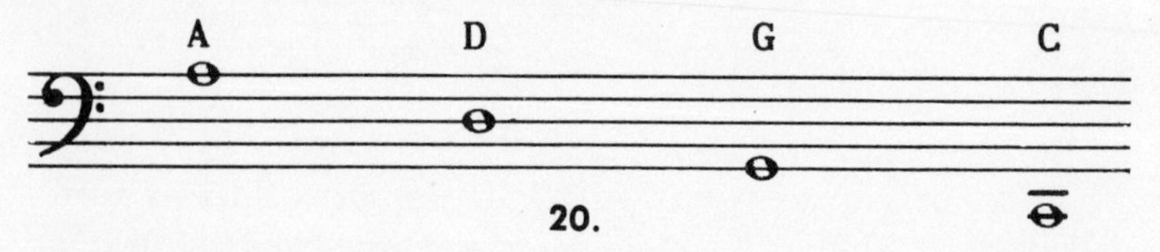

20.

There are usually about 10 cellists in the symphony orchestra. The cello is also an important instrument in the string quartet where it is the lowest-sounding instrument. Often, too, it's used as a solo instrument.

Suggested Recordings

Beethoven: *Symphony No. 5* – Andante (Second Movement
Brahms: *Symphony No. 3* – Third Movement
Nevin: *A Day in Venice*
Saint-Saëns: *Carnival of the Animals* (The Swan)

21. The cello is large, so you balance it between your knees with the tailpin on the floor.

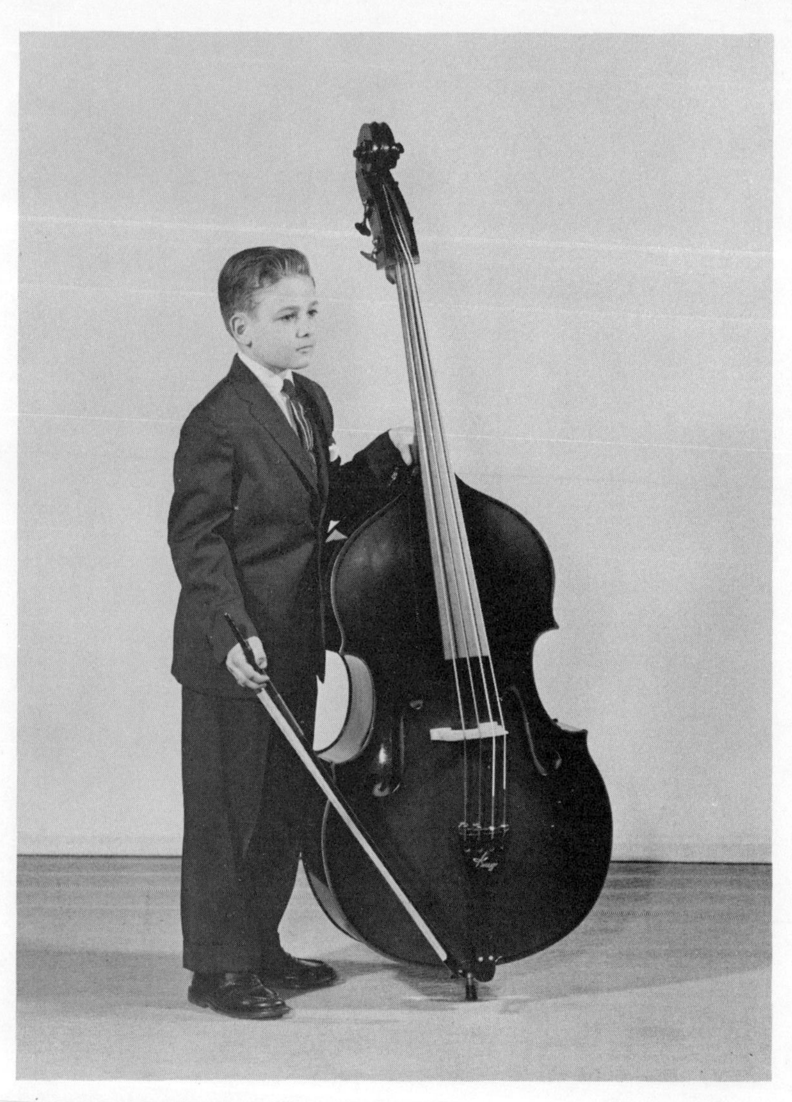

22. The double bass is the giant of the string family. To play it, stand it on its tailpin and hold it with your left hand.

Double Bass

Because of its size, the double bass is always an eye-catching instrument in the orchestra. It's the lowest-sounding of the string family and is known variously as string bass, bass or bass viol. Bass players play their instruments either from a standing position or sitting on a high stool.

Two types of bows are used for the double bass: the French bow, similar to the cello bow and held in the same manner; and the German bow which is wider and longer than the French bow and held quite differently.

Since bass strings are very thick and heavy, ordinary pegs for tightening or loosening the strings, such as you find on the other three string instruments, cannot be used. Instead, you have keys connected to a gear. This gear turns a metal rod which holds the strings. The gear allows you to tighten or loosen the bass strings with very little effort and there's no possibility of the strings slipping.

The strings of the bass are tuned to the following notes:

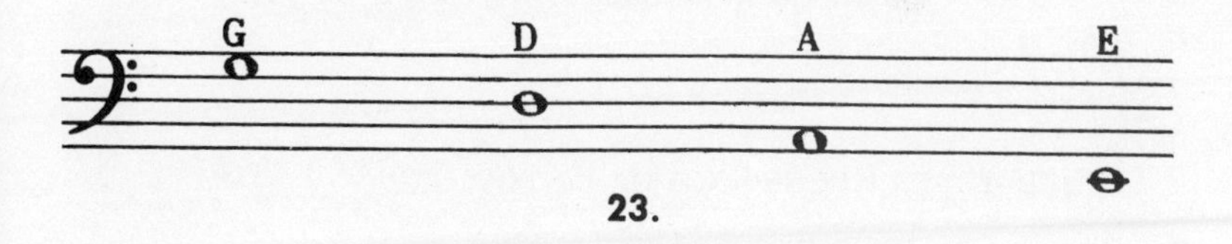

23.

You see as many as 10 to 12 double basses in a full symphony orchestra and also find them in many concert bands. The bass plays an important part in all dance bands, small or large, where the player plays pizzicato (plucks with his fingers) most of the time. The double bass is rarely used as a solo instrument in the orchestra or concert band but frequently it has solo parts in jazz. Listen for the double bass in the following recordings.

Suggested Recordings

Bach-Stokowski: *Prelude in B Minor*
Beethoven: *Symphony No. 5* – Third Movement
Saint-Saëns: *Carnival of the Animals* (The Elephant)
Schubert: *Symphony No. 8, The Unfinished* – First Movement

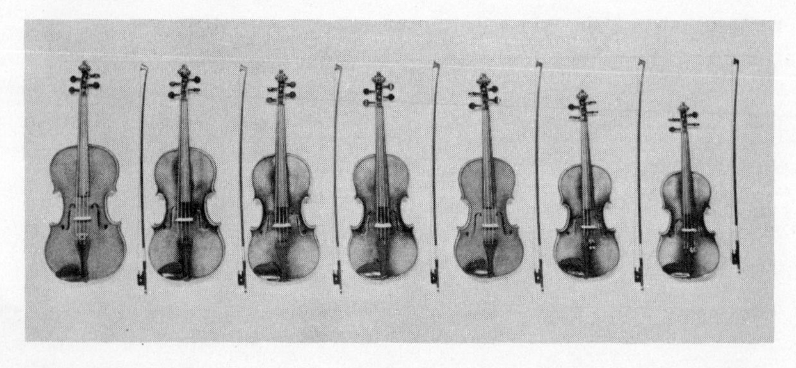

24. Violins come in many different sizes. If it is your choice, pick the size that is most comfortable for you.

Suggested Recordings of Entire String Family

Bach: *Suite in D*
Mozart: *Eine Kleine Nachtmusik*
Tschaikowsky: *Symphony No. 4* – Third Movement

The string family is a very harmonious one and a great deal of beautiful music has been written for string quartets or string ensembles (larger groups). If you and some other members of your family or some of your close friends learn to play the various strings, you can have a lot of fun and pleasure playing together.

OTHER STRINGS

Harp

The harp is the oldest of the string instruments and it may possibly be the oldest instrument in existence. Yet the present-day harp goes back only about 150 years. As early as 1300 B.C., the Egyptians played on a harp-like instrument, and the ancient Greeks had the lyre, but all these early instruments had only a few strings and therefore only a few notes could be played.

For many centuries the harp remained an incomplete instrument because a player couldn't produce many notes. When more strings were added, the instrument became too large and too difficult to play. Some kind of mechanism was needed to provide the harp with all the necessary notes without adding more strings.

The answer was pedals. Pedals were added to the harp in the 18th century, and this allowed the player to produce all the needed notes. More and more pedals were added until one harp maker constructed a harp with 14 pedals! This instrument could produce all the needed notes, but the harp again became too difficult to play.

Near the beginning of the 19th century, Sebastian Erard, a famous piano maker, solved the problem by reducing the number of pedals to seven, the same number as we have on the harp today. Each pedal controls one note of the musical scale—one pedal controls all the A's, another all the B's, etc. These pedals, which look like piano pedals,

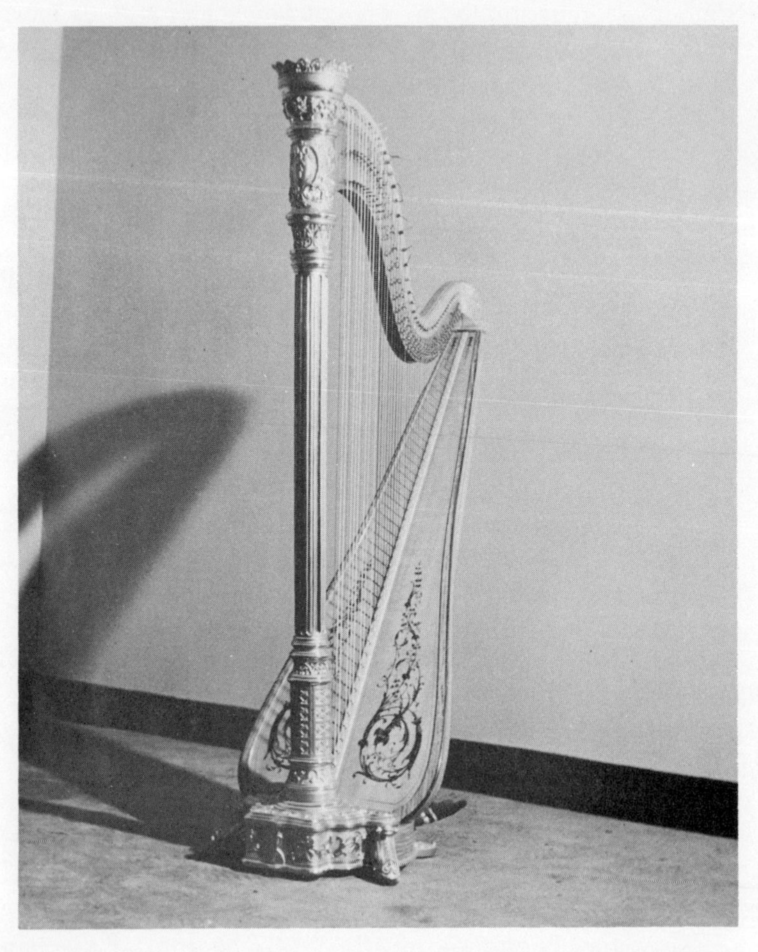

25. The stately harp has a sound as lovely as its appearance.

can shorten or lengthen the string to give different pitches. In this way the harp with 47 strings can produce all the necessary notes—almost as many as the piano.

To play the harp, you tilt the instrument toward you as you sit, with the top of the harp body over your right shoulder. You pluck the strings, which causes them to vibrate and produce sounds. The soundboard and hollow body of the instrument increase the sound.

The harp is a beautiful instrument, both in appearance and sound. It has a graceful hollow pillar which contains the pedal rods. The top of the harp, called the neck, curves to provide a shorter space for the shorter strings.

At least one harp is used in the symphony orchestra. It is widely used as a solo instrument and also in some chamber music groups, together with other strings and woodwinds.

SUGGESTED RECORDINGS

Delibes: *Pizzicato from "Sylvia"*
Salzedo: *Short Stories for the Harpist*
Tschaikowsky: *The Nutcracker Suite* (Valse of the Flowers)

Guitar

If you go into a music store to buy a guitar, you will be amazed to see the many different sizes and shapes that are available. Over three centuries ago, a bass guitar called the chitarron was seven feet tall and had eight pairs of strings. The lute, another ancient guitar-like instrument, was pear-shaped with a long fretted fingerboard. The six-string guitar developed in the 17th century has been the most popular guitar, right up to the present time.

It had frets on the fingerboard and wooden tuning

26. The classic guitar, used by concert guitarists, has six strings made of nylon, with three of them wound with fine wire.

pegs, but since the invention of the modern Spanish guitar, metal screws have replaced the wooden pegs to make tuning easier.

The Spanish guitar is one of the basic guitars used today. There are two types of Spanish guitars, classic and steel-string. The classic guitar is the original Spanish guitar and is the instrument used by our concert guitarists. It has six strings made of nylon with the three lower strings wound with fine wire. Many people think that the guitar is used only for folk songs, cowboy tunes and rock-and-roll. This isn't true at all. Such great composers as Berlioz and Schubert included guitar parts in some of their compositions.

The steel-string guitar was introduced in the 1920's. Although it resembles the classic guitar in appearance, it has a narrower fingerboard, steel strings, and an end pin on which the player ties a neck cord. Whenever you see a guitar player supporting his instrument by a cord around his neck, you will know he's using a steel-string Spanish guitar. The guitars with different shapes you see displayed in the music stores are also all steel-string guitars, as the classic guitar does not have this variety in shape. You use the steel-string guitar for accompanying singing and in the dance band.

You play the classic guitar in either a sitting or standing position with the left foot raised and supported by a small stool. You rest the instrument on the left leg and press it lightly against the body with the right arm. With the steel-string guitar, you don't need the stool as the neck cord supports the instrument. When the instrument is in position, you pluck the strings with the fingers of your right hand or with a plectrum (pick) while the fingers of your left hand (the thumb is not used) press the strings against the fingerboard to play the notes. If you use a plectrum, hold it be-

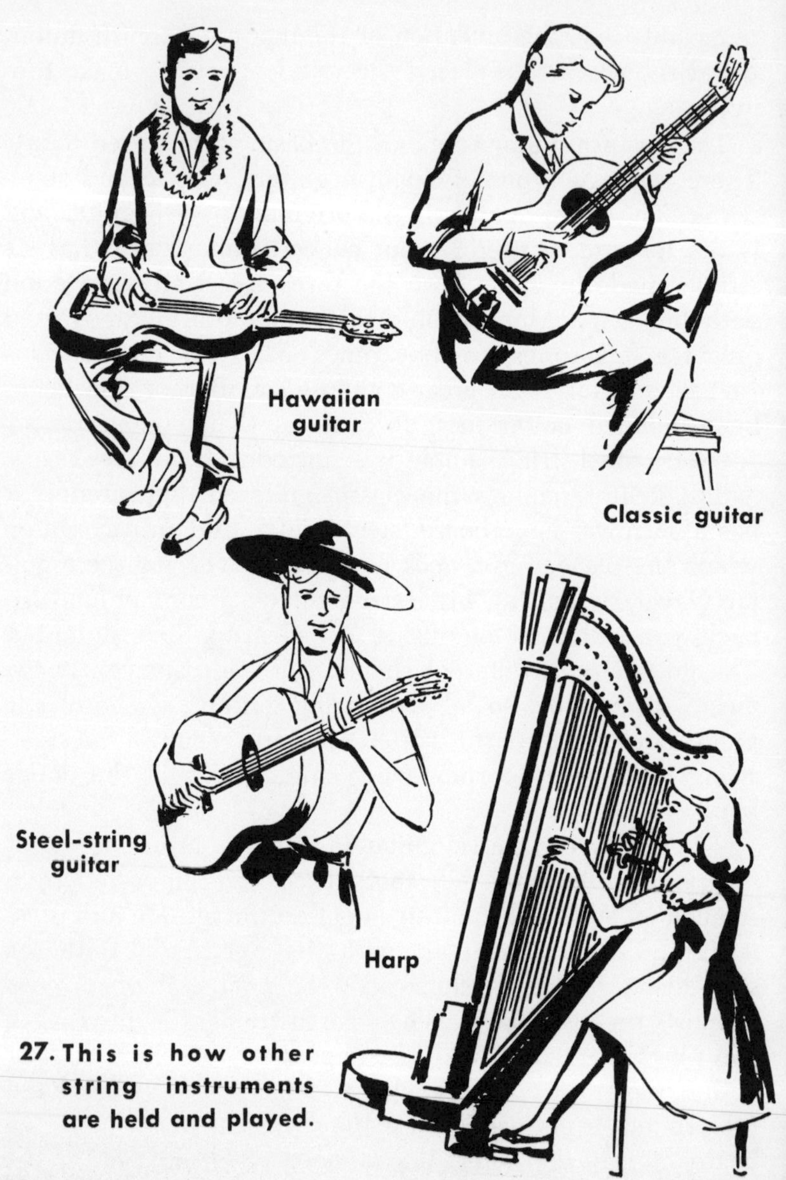

27. This is how other string instruments are held and played.

tween the thumb and forefinger with the smaller end picking the strings.

All Spanish guitars can be made to sound louder by the use of electricity. You attach a small pick-up (microphone) to the instrument and this is connected to an amplifier. In this way, the instrument can be heard even with a large band.

The Hawaiian guitar is an amplified steel guitar. You play it in a sitting position with the instrument resting on your lap. With this guitar, you use a thumb pick and two or three finger picks which fit on the fingers like rings. You move a steel bar, which you hold in your left hand, up and down the fingerboard to get the notes you want to play. A special effect called a glide can be produced by first plucking and then sliding the bar over the top of the strings. This guitar is used primarily for playing Hawaiian music.

Suggested Recordings

Paganini: *Sonata No. 11 for Violin and Guitar*
Tarrega: *Gran Jota*
Tarrega: *Estudio in A Major*
Turina: *Fandanguillo*

4. THE WOODWINDS

Did you know that primitive man made the first woodwind instrument? He cut a hollow piece of wood and blew air through it to make a sound. He found that if he blew through a longer hollow piece of wood, he got a different sound. Then by cutting a hole in the side of the wood and blowing, he produced a higher sound. As the years went by, men added more holes and discovered they could make different sounds by covering or opening the holes. These were our earliest woodwind instruments. The recorder that we see today is very much like them. (The recorder is discussed in Chapter 7.)

So the word "woodwind" simply means wind passing through a hollow piece of wood. Originally, all woodwind instruments were made of wood. Within the past 100 years, however, the flute and piccolo have been made of metal, and a new woodwind was invented which is not made of wood. The saxophone is a cross between a woodwind and a brass. Because it is similar to the clarinet, it is usually included among the woodwinds. The clarinet, oboe, bassoon and English horn are other members of the woodwind family.

We know from the discussion of the string family that the larger the instrument, the lower the pitch; and the smaller the instrument, the higher the pitch. The same principle applies to the woodwinds—the bassoon, for example, is 109 inches in length and has a deep low sound like a foghorn; while the piccolo, smallest of the woodwinds, has a very high pitch, sometimes resembling the chirping of a bird.

You produce musical sounds on a woodwind by blowing into the instrument, causing a column of air to vibrate. When you close all the holes of a woodwind instrument, you get the lowest pitch of that instrument. As you open additional holes from the bottom, the sound becomes higher and higher. This is because the air escaping from the first open hole makes the air column shorter. In other words, the shorter the column of air, the higher the pitch, and the longer the column of air, the lower the pitch.

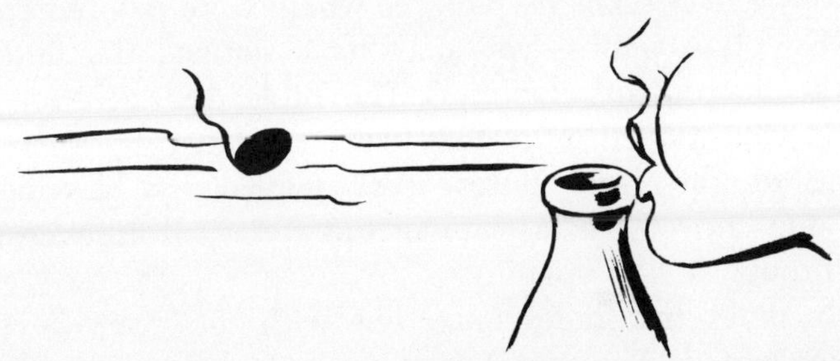

28. You can see how a woodwind instrument works by blowing across a bottle.

Try this simple experiment: Blow air across the top of an empty soda bottle by placing the bottle under your lower lip. Stretch your lips and smile, leaving just a small opening in the center (see Illus. 28). Blow easily between the lips. Listen to the sound it makes. Now try the same thing on a larger bottle. Listen again. What was the difference in the two sounds? You heard a lower sound coming from the larger bottle.

You can do the same experiment using just one bottle. Blow across the top, then pour some water into the bottle and blow again. What do you hear? Keep adding more water and blowing each time. You will notice the sound getting higher and higher as more water is added. This is because you are shortening the air column inside the bottle.

Since there are more holes on a woodwind instrument than fingers on your two hands, round coverings which open and close more than one hole at a time were invented. These coverings are called keys.

Now let's discuss each instrument in the woodwind family.

Flute and Piccolo

If you've ever seen the pictures which were painted on ancient Egyptian tombs, you may have noticed the flute among the instruments depicted. The Bible, too, mentions shepherds who played on a flute-like instrument.

Some of the early flutes were played by blowing through one end of the instrument but today all flutes are played through a side opening.

Early flutes had holes only, but with the years keys have been added. The metal flute we now know was developed in 1847 by Theobald Boehm, a noted German flutist. Boehm took the best parts of all the flutes of his time and combined them into one. He was the one who changed the flute from wood to metal. He also changed the shape of

29. To play the flute, you blow into the open hole on top while you press the keys.

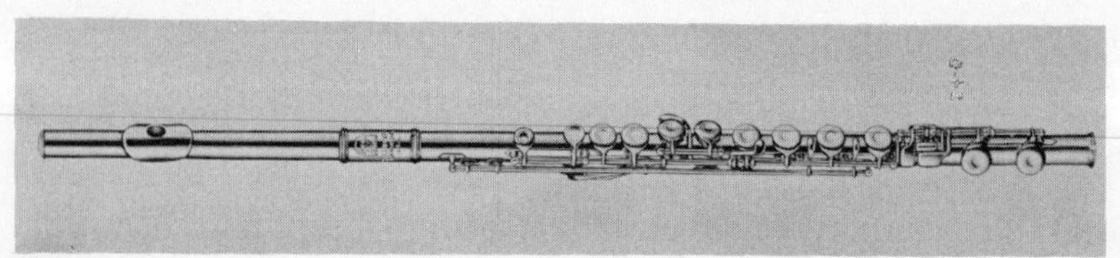

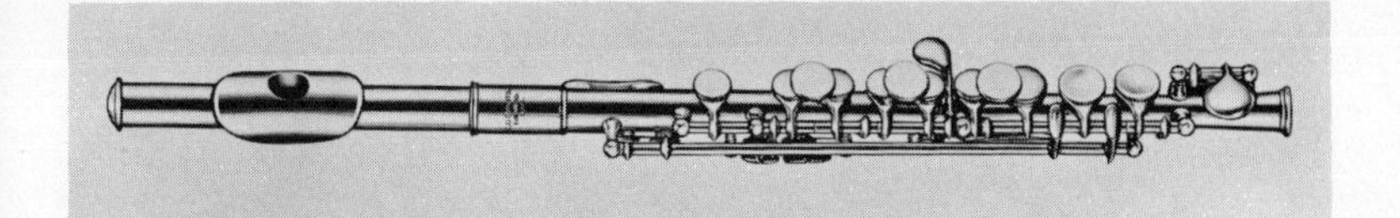

30. The piccolo, which has a very high-pitched sound, is like a baby flute.

the instrument from conical (like a cone) to cylindrical (like a straight pipe).

The flute and piccolo are the highest-pitched instruments of the woodwind family, and the only instruments of the group which are played without reeds.

You can see only one hole in the flute and piccolo in the pictures. The other holes are all hidden under the keys. The opening you see on the side near the top is the blow-hole. When you blow across and into it, the air inside vibrates. This vibration causes the sound. You use the keys to play a tune, but of course you must learn which keys to operate. There are also open-hole flutes. Here the holes are in the keys, and when you cover a hole, you operate a key at the same time.

You play the flute by placing the opening of the mouthpiece just below your lower lip, in the same way as you blew across the bottle. Be sure to stretch your lips. This is most important, because the corners of your mouth must be tightly closed, with a small opening in the center to allow the air to come out in a small steady stream. This formation of the lips is called the *embouchure*. When a musician refers to his "lip," he means the *embouchure*—one of the essential principles of playing any brass or woodwind instrument. Unless you form your lips properly, you cannot make a correct sound.

It's like pinching and stretching the opening of a

31. This is how you hold the different woodwind instruments.

blown-up balloon. When you allow air to escape gradually, you can control the sound that comes out. But if you just release the balloon, all you hear is a swooshing sound of air escaping at once with a rush.

In the same way, when playing the flute or piccolo, it is absolutely necessary to allow a thin, steady stream of air to pass through the small opening in order to produce a good tone from your instrument.

The piccolo, a product of the late 18th and early 19th centuries, is like a baby flute and played the same way. Its high sound stands out even when all instruments in an orchestra are playing. The flute and piccolo are so much alike that the flutist often plays the piccolo too.

There are two or three flutes in the symphony orchestra. One or more of the flute players also plays the piccolo. This is called doubling, and simply means a player can play either instrument, depending upon the music. Both instruments are also used in the concert and marching bands. You also see flutes in small groups which play chamber music, and they are becoming increasingly popular in the dance band.

Suggested Recordings

Flute:

Creston: *The Incredible Flutist*
Debussy: *Afternoon of a Faun* – Prelude
Prokofiev: *Peter and the Wolf* (the part of the bird)
Saint-Saëns: *Carnival of the Animals* (The Birds)
Tschaikowsky: *The Nutcracker Suite* (Dance of the Flutes)

Piccolo:

Kleinsinger: *Peewee the Piccolo*
Sousa: *Stars and Stripes Forever*—piccolo solo
Tschaikowsky: *The Nutcracker Suite* (Chinese Dance)

32. This B-flat clarinet is the most widely played

Clarinet

Pictures of ancient Egyptian tombs also reveal musicians playing an instrument which looks like two wooden pipes tied together. Today, after thousands of years, people in some Arabic countries still play the same type of early clarinet.

Like the flute, the early clarinet had no keys to cover the holes. In 1690, Johann Denner added keys and in 1843 Hyacinth Klosé, a great clarinetist, contributed the most important improvement. He added the Boehm system of rings, very similar to the ring system of the flute. He also wrote a clarinet-instruction book which introduced his new fingering system. If you should decide to study the clarinet, you will probably study from a Klosé book.

The clarinet is a cylindrical instrument with a conical bell. Most clarinets are made of grenadilla wood but you'll also find some of ebonite, metal or hard rubber. The wooden clarinet is made up of five separate parts: the mouthpiece, tuning barrel, upper joint, lower joint and the bell.

We call the clarinet a single-reed instrument. A reed is a piece of cane (a kind of wood that resembles the bamboo) shaped as shown in the illustration. It is attached to

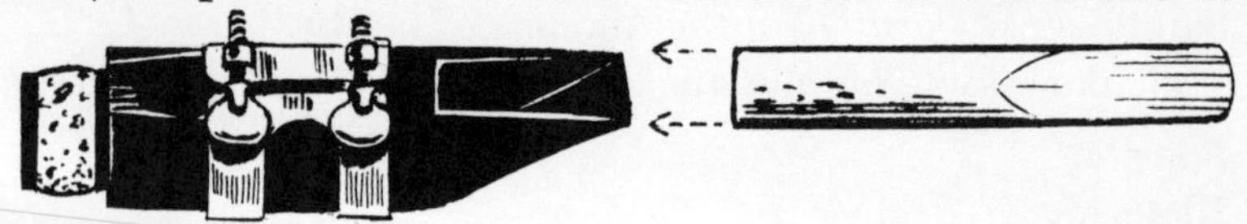

33. A reed of cane is attached to the clarinet's mouthpiece with a ligature.

the mouthpiece by means of a clamp called a ligature (see Illus. 33). You produce a sound by blowing air through the opening between the reed and the mouthpiece. When you do this, the thin tip of the reed vibrates, which in turn vibrates the column of air in the tube.

Just blowing the clarinet sounds simple, but here is what you must actually do to produce a sound:

1. Smile and stretch your lips—to form the *embouchure*.
2. Place your bottom lip slightly over your bottom teeth so that the lip acts as a cushion for the reed.
3. Place about one-half inch or more (amount differs with each individual) of the mouthpiece in your mouth with the reed resting on your lower lip.
4. Rest your top teeth on the top of the mouthpiece.
5. Close the corners of your lips.
6. Blow easily into the mouthpiece, allowing the tip of the reed to vibrate.

If, after all that, you make no sound (which often happens), then you are pressing the reed too hard and preventing it from vibrating. Loosen the pressure a bit and try again.

There are different kinds of clarinets but the one most commonly played is the B-flat clarinet. Another widely used type is the bass clarinet which curves at the top and at the bottom. The largest clarinet, which has the lowest sound, is the double bass, but you will rarely see this played. The A clarinet is used only in the symphony orchestra and the E-flat clarinet is also less frequently heard.

The clarinet is a popular, important instrument in all kinds of musical groups. It is the heart of the concert and marching band, just as the violins are the heart of the orchestra. Symphony orchestras use the clarinet and so do woodwind groups which play chamber music (classical music written for small groups of instruments). Dance bands both large and small feature the clarinet. The reason it is so widely used is because you can play notes rapidly or very slowly with it. You can produce special sounds—harsh or shrill, loud, soft or mellow—and it blends well with other instruments. In short, the clarinet is a versatile instrument—an instrument of many uses.

SUGGESTED RECORDINGS

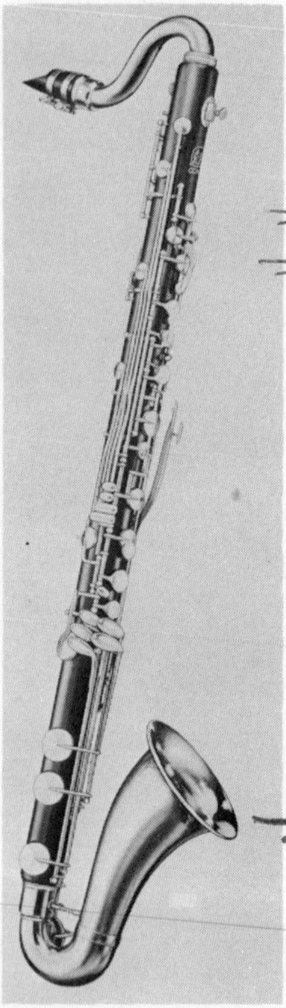

B-flat Clarinet:

Copland: *El Salon Mexico*
Enesco: *Roumanian Rhapsody*
Mozart: *Quintet for Clarinet and Strings*
Prokofiev: *Peter and the Wolf* (The Cat)
Saint-Saëns: *Carnival of the Animals* (Cuckoo)
Schubert: *Unfinished Symphony*
Wagner: *Overture to Tannhäuser*
Weber: *Overture to Oberon*

Bass Clarinet:

Grofé: *Grand Canyon Suite* (On the Trail)
Tschaikowsky: *The Nutcracker Suite* (Sugar Plum Fairy)
Wagner: *Siegfried's Rhine Journey*

E-flat Clarinet:

Gershwin: *Rhapsody in Blue*
Ravel: *Bolero*

34. The bass clarinet curves at the top and bottom. As its name suggests, it has a low sound

Saxophone

The saxophone is a very special instrument. Other instruments developed gradually over a long period of time. The saxophone hasn't changed since it was invented! In 1840, Adolph Sax did something which students in a music classroom sometimes do when the teacher is not present. He put a clarinet mouthpiece on a brass instrument and blew through it. The brass instrument sounded like a woodwind! To this, Sax added keys—and the saxophone was born.

35. (Left) Tenor saxophone (Right) Baritone saxophone

36. Different types of saxophones

E-flat alto

B-flat tenor

E-flat baritone

The instrument produced a new sound, powerful, rich and mellow.

You play the saxophone in much the same way as you do the clarinet, so if you learn to play one, you'll probably learn the other. Most saxophone players who play in dance bands "double" on the clarinet.

Saxophones, like the clarinets, differ in size, and for each size you need a different mouthpiece. The larger the instrument, the larger the mouthpiece. The most commonly

37. Alto saxophone

used saxophones are the E-flat alto, B-flat tenor and the E-flat baritone. There are three other saxophones, the B-flat soprano, C melody and B-flat bass, but they are rarely played now.

We sometimes see the saxophone in a symphony orchestra but of course symphonic music written before its invention did not include saxophone parts. However, more and more modern composers write parts for this instrument so that in the future, the saxophone may become a regular member of the symphony orchestra.

The saxophone blends well with both the brass and woodwind groups. Because of this, it plays a prominent role in all types of bands. School orchestras today usually include saxophonists and you know, of course, that it is a key member of most jazz groups.

Suggested Recordings

Bizet: *L'Arlesienne Suite* (Prelude)
Creston: *Suite for Saxophone and Piano*
Creston: *Sonata for Saxophone*
Creston: *Concerto for Saxophone and Orchestra*
Debussy: *Rhapsody for Saxophone and Orchestra*
Ibert: *Concertino da Camera*
Shostakovich: *Golden Age* (Polka)—for Tenor Sax

DOUBLE-REED WOODWIND INSTRUMENTS

Many centuries ago, the Crusaders who reached the Orient were intrigued by a double-reed instrument made of two hollow pieces of wood called a shawm. They brought it back to Europe with them and over the centuries it underwent many changes. From these improvements the oboe, English horn and bassoon took shape.

The oboe, English horn and bassoon are called double-reed instruments because their mouthpieces consist of two separate pieces of cane, a bamboo-like wood. The two pieces are tied together back to back with a slight opening between them to allow air to pass through. As you blow through the opening, both reeds vibrate. This vibration sets the air column into motion and produces a sound.

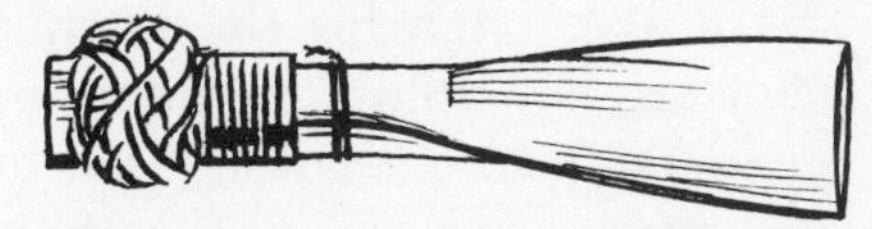

38. Two pieces of cane, tied together, make up a double reed. An oboe reed is above, bassoon below.

You can purchase a reed for your particular instrument at any music store, but most professional musicians prefer to make their own reed.

For a double-reed *embouchure,* you must form a cushion with both your upper and lower lips by placing them over the teeth—just as you do when you drink through a straw.

To illustrate the double-reed principle, try this simple experiment (see Illus. 39).

Take an ordinary drinking straw. Flatten one end and

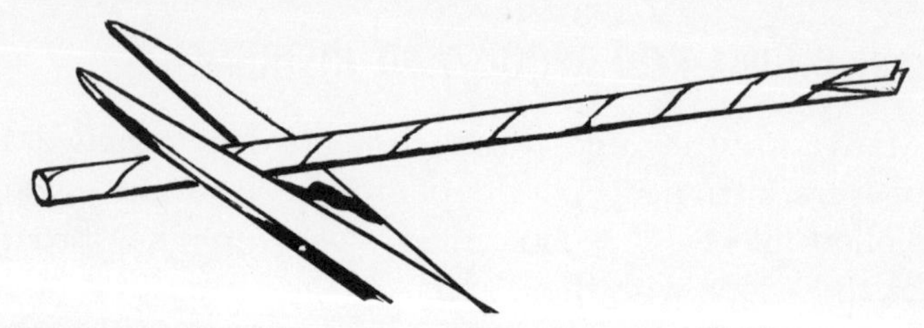

39. A simple experiment with a straw will illustrate the double-reed principle.

cut the flattened corners with a pair of scissors. This forms an opening similar to a double reed. Place this end between your lips and blow lightly. You should produce a sound, caused by the vibration of each flattened side of the straw. Now cut the bottom of the straw and blow again. You will find that the sound is higher.

Oboe and English Horn

The oboe is the soprano of the double-reed group. It is the tuning pitch for the symphony orchestra. Because the oboe cannot adjust its pitch as well as any of the other instruments, it *gives* the pitch to the other members of the orchestra.

It's a mystery why the English horn is called by that name, because it is not a horn and was not developed in England. The English horn might be considered an alto oboe—it is about 8 inches longer than the oboe and therefore its pitch is lower. The English horn has a slightly bent mouthpiece to allow the player to play in a comfortable position. Also, its bell (the end piece) is pear-shaped while the oboe has a conventional bell.

Many oboists play the English horn as well, since they are played in much the same way. There are generally three oboe players in the symphony orchestra and concert band. One of these players will also play the English horn.

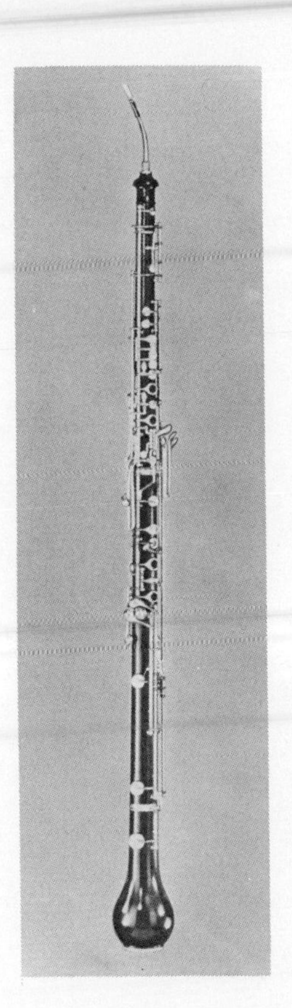

40.

(Left) Oboe
(Right) English horn

Suggested Recordings

Oboe:

Bach: *Sinfonia to Church Cantata No. 156*
Bach: *Jesu, Joy of Man's Desiring*
Offenbach: *Orpheus in the Underworld*
Prokofiev: *Peter and the Wolf* (Duck)
Satie-Debussy: *Gympodie*

English Horn:

Bach-Stokowski: *Fugue in G Minor* (Little Fugue)
Dvorak: *New World Symphony* (Slow Movement)
Franck: *Symphony in D Minor* (Second Movement)
Sibelius: *The Swan of Tuonela*

41. When you blow into a bassoon, the air goes down one pipe and travels up the other.

Bassoon

The bassoon, the bass of the double-reed group, was originally a large bass shawm. In the Middle Ages it was extremely long—sometimes over 8 feet—so that it could produce low pitches. By the 16th century, it was shortened by means of two wooden cylinders placed side by side and connected in a "U" shape.

Our modern bassoon is also "U"-shaped (see Illus. 41) but with additional keys and rings. It's still long, however—over 9 feet—but you would never guess the actual length because of the way it is put together, and the total length

42. Double-reed woodwinds

Oboe

English horn

Bassoon

of the contra-bassoon is 16 feet! The picture shows that the instrument is made of a double pipe. The air goes down one pipe, makes a U-turn and goes up the other pipe. Only in this way could one person handle this large, low-pitched woodwind instrument. A cord placed around the player's neck hooks on to the bassoon and helps to support it. The bassoon's bell points upward. The contra-bassoon, a very large bassoon, is the lowest-sounding instrument of the woodwind family. Its bell points downward.

There are at least three bassoons in the symphony orchestra and concert band.

Suggested Recordings

Bassoon:

Prokofiev: *Peter and the Wolf* (Grandpa)
Rimsky-Korsakov: *Scheherazade* (Second Movement)
Rossini: *Barber of Seville Overture*
Tschaikowsky: *Symphony No. 6* (First Movement)

Contra-Bassoon:

Dukas: *The Sorcerer's Apprentice*
Taylor: *Looking-Glass Suite* (Jabberwocky)

Suggested Recordings of Entire Woodwind Family

Goldmark: *Rustic Wedding Symphony* (First Movement)
Mendelssohn: *A Midsummer Night's Dream* (Scherzo)
Wagner: *Overture to Tannhäuser*

5. THE BRASS

To frighten away evil spirits, primitive people blew instruments made from the horns and tusks of animals. These horns were rough and harsh-sounding. The shofar still used today in certain religious ceremonies is a ram's horn typical of these ancient instruments.

Gradually metal was substituted for horns and tusks, and different people devised instruments of silver or brass. The Jews played a trumpet called the hasosro, a straight metal tube made of silver. The Greeks had the salpinx, a tube containing 13 sections of ivory fitted into one another and held together by bronze rings. The Romans developed a small instrument which they called the tuba (not to be confused with the modern-day tuba which is a very large brass instrument). The Roman tuba was a conical bronze tube approximately 4 feet long. Also of bronze was the Nordic lurer, an interesting double trumpet that could be played separately or together. Some musicians in India still play this type of horn.

The ancient instruments could produce only a few notes and they were so long they were clumsy to handle. They were not used to make music but rather they were for signalling, religious or military purposes.

The first big change in the early brass instrument was the shape.

Because the long straight horn was too difficult to manage, someone got the idea of coiling the metal tube. The same length of tubing was used but the new shape was easier to handle. However, the instruments still sounded only a few notes like the bugle.

Various devices were tried to increase the number of notes. Finally in 1815, the valve instrument was invented. These valves enable the player to lengthen the instrument by simply pressing a piston (a metal piece which moves up and down in a cylinder). The piston controls the length of tubing and makes it possible to produce all the necessary notes on the horn. Since the valves are such an important part of brass instruments, let us see how they work.

When you do not press any valves, the air you blow into the instrument passes only through the main tube. When you press a valve down, the air must pass through additional tubing and the sound becomes lower. Each of the three valves controls a different section of tubing. When you press down all the valves, you are using all the tubing of the instrument.

When you release a valve, it automatically returns to its normal position and that section of tubing is again closed off from the main tube. This type of valve, the piston valve, is used on all brass instruments except the French horn and some tubas which use rotary valves.

43. The mouthpieces, from left to right, are for a French horn, mellophone and alto horn, cornet, trumpet, baritone horn, E-flat bass (tuba) and BB-flat bass (tuba).

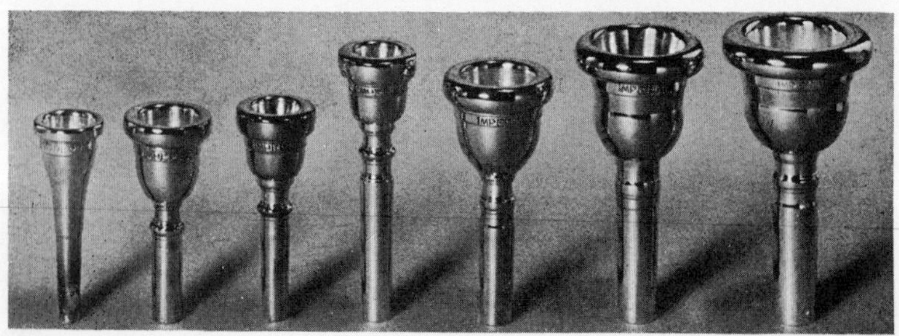

The rotary valve performs the same work as the piston valve but by a different method. A rotary valve is a disc about the size of a 25-cent piece. When you press a lever the rotary flips to open additional tubing. When you release the lever, the rotary springs back to its normal position, closing that portion of tubing.

Modern brass instruments are all made of metal and all use metal cup-shaped mouthpieces except the French horn, whose mouthpiece resembles a small funnel. You can't play a brass blowing instrument without a mouthpiece, and the mouthpiece must fit your particular needs to enable you to produce good tone.

The vibration of the lips in the mouthpiece produces the sound from a mouthpiece instrument. This vibration in turn causes the air in the tubing to vibrate, which reinforces the sound and sets the pitch. The following experiment demonstrates how vibration produces sound:

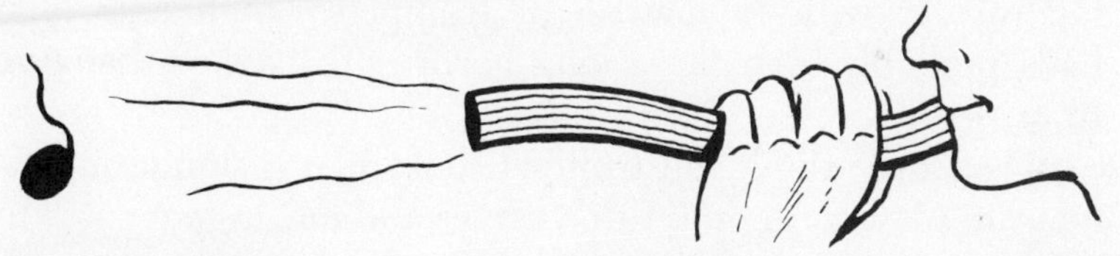

44. You will get a horn-like sound by blowing into a hose.

Find a short piece of old garden hose or bathroom shower hose and wash it clean so that you can put it to your mouth. Now form your lips by stretching them and smiling. Then blow air through the lips, vibrating them, and try to get a buzzing sound. Now place your mouth to one end of the hose (if you use a bathroom shower hose, the end that normally fits onto the faucet can serve as your mouthpiece) and blow the same way. You should get a horn-like sound. If you have different lengths of hose, you can blow into each and produce different pitches.

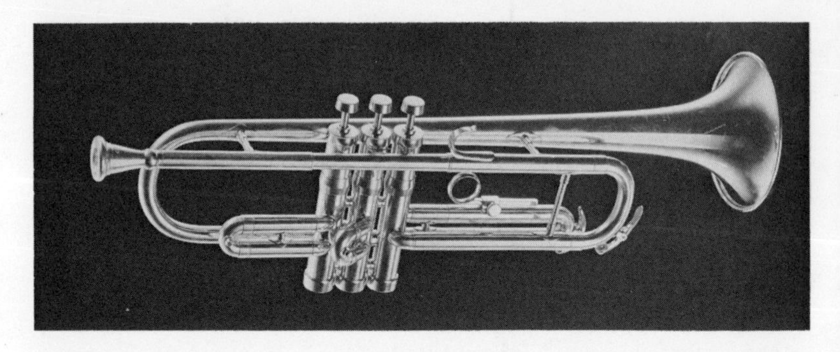

45. The trumpet looks simpler to play than it is. The three valves, alone and in combination, produce many notes.

Trumpet and Cornet

The trumpet and cornet are exciting instruments both to hear and to play. From Biblical times onward, their loud sound has been ideal for military purposes and for announcing royalty with "a flourish of trumpets." In movies, you have probably seen these long horns with banners hanging from them.

You may think the trumpet looks like a simple instrument to play, with only three valves and only a few notes to learn. However, it isn't that simple. Each valve and each combination of valves allows a whole series of notes to be played, and there are many notes to be learned after all.

At one time, the early trumpet was played only by men, and in some tribes, a woman caught viewing a trumpet was put to death. Today, of course, both boys and girls, men and women play the trumpet. You see the trumpet in the marching band, concert band, dance band, and of course, in the symphony orchestra where it occupies an important place. Generally two to four are used in an orchestra. The cornet is not nearly as widely used as the trumpet. It is primarily heard with concert and marching bands and sometimes as a solo instrument.

The cornet looks smaller than the trumpet but if you were to stretch out the tubing of both instruments, you'd find them the same length, approximately 4½ feet. Because of their coiled shape, you would never believe their tubing is so long. Since both instruments are of the same length, you can play either one, using exactly the same music.

The trumpet is the highest-pitched instrument of the brass family. You can play the trumpet at any tempo, very slow to very fast, and produce a wide range of tones—from very soft and sweet to very loud and brilliant. By using various types of mutes, you can create many special effects

46. The cornet is similar to the trumpet, but looks a little smaller.

with the trumpet. A mute, if you recall, is a device used on certain instruments to change the tone quality. With the trumpet, you place the mute in the bell. See the picture of various types of mutes commonly used.

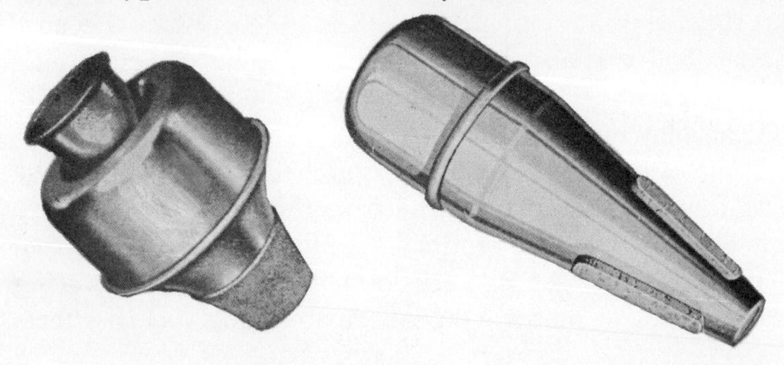

47. A mute in the bell of a trumpet changes the instrument's tone.

To make a sound on the trumpet, you do the following:

Set your lips for playing by first smiling, then stretching them. Leave a small opening in the center of the lips. Blow lightly through the lip opening and buzz your lips but avoid puffing your cheeks. A slight smile will help you avoid this. To make a higher sound, stretch your lips a bit more.

You can practice lip buzzing with just the mouthpiece. When you think you've succeeded on the mouthpiece, put it back on the instrument and try producing a trumpet tone. It's often harder than you'd think. To produce *any* sound on the trumpet can be difficult! If you choose to play this exciting instrument, you will need a qualified teacher to help you play properly.

If you decide to learn to play either of these instruments, it will be on the B-flat cornet or trumpet, the most common type. Those pitched in other keys are used less frequently.

Suggested Recordings

Bizet: *Carmen Suite* (Changing of the Guard)
Grofé: *Grand Canyon Suite* (On the Trail)
Prokofiev: *Peter and the Wolf* (Hunter)
Shostakovitch: *Polka from The Age of Gold Ballet*
Verdi: *Aida* (Triumphal March)
Wagner: *Tannhäuser* (Second Act)

French Horn

The French horn consists of a long cone-shaped metal tube with a narrow, funnel-shaped mouthpiece at one end

48. The single French horn has about 12 feet of tubing, but it's all coiled up.

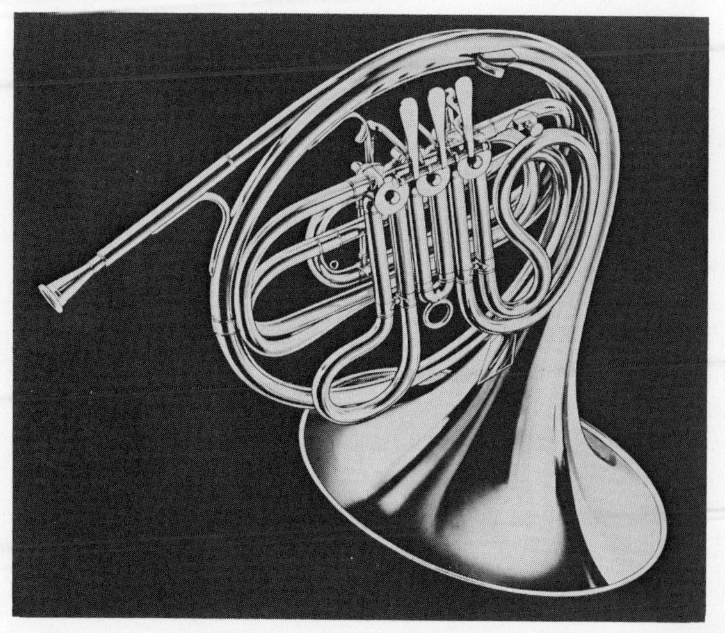

49. The double French horn plays in F, but a valve converts it to E-flat.

and a flaring bell at the other. Nobody knows why this instrument is called a French horn.

Two types of horns are in common use: the double French horn used in the modern orchestra, and the single horn. The double French horn is an F horn, but when you press a special valve, it becomes a B-flat horn. That's why it's called a double horn; actually, two horns in one. This enables the player to play more notes than he could otherwise. The double French horn has 16 feet of coiled tubing. The single horn, also in F, has about 12 feet of tubing. By adding a slide (an extra piece of tubing) this horn becomes an E-flat horn. So in a sense, it, too, is a double horn.

You play the French horn by buzzing your lips against the mouthpiece, which, as was pointed out earlier, is different from other brass instrument mouthpieces (like a small funnel). Unlike the other brasses, however, you operate the valves of the French horn with the fingers of your left hand. You place your right hand in the bell with the fingers extended into the horn to help support the instrument and to play in tune. This also acts as a kind of mute.

The double French horn is a very important instrument in the orchestra and band because it blends well with the other groups of instruments and has the widest range of notes of all brass and woodwind instruments.

50. The mellophone resembles the French horn but its sound is different.

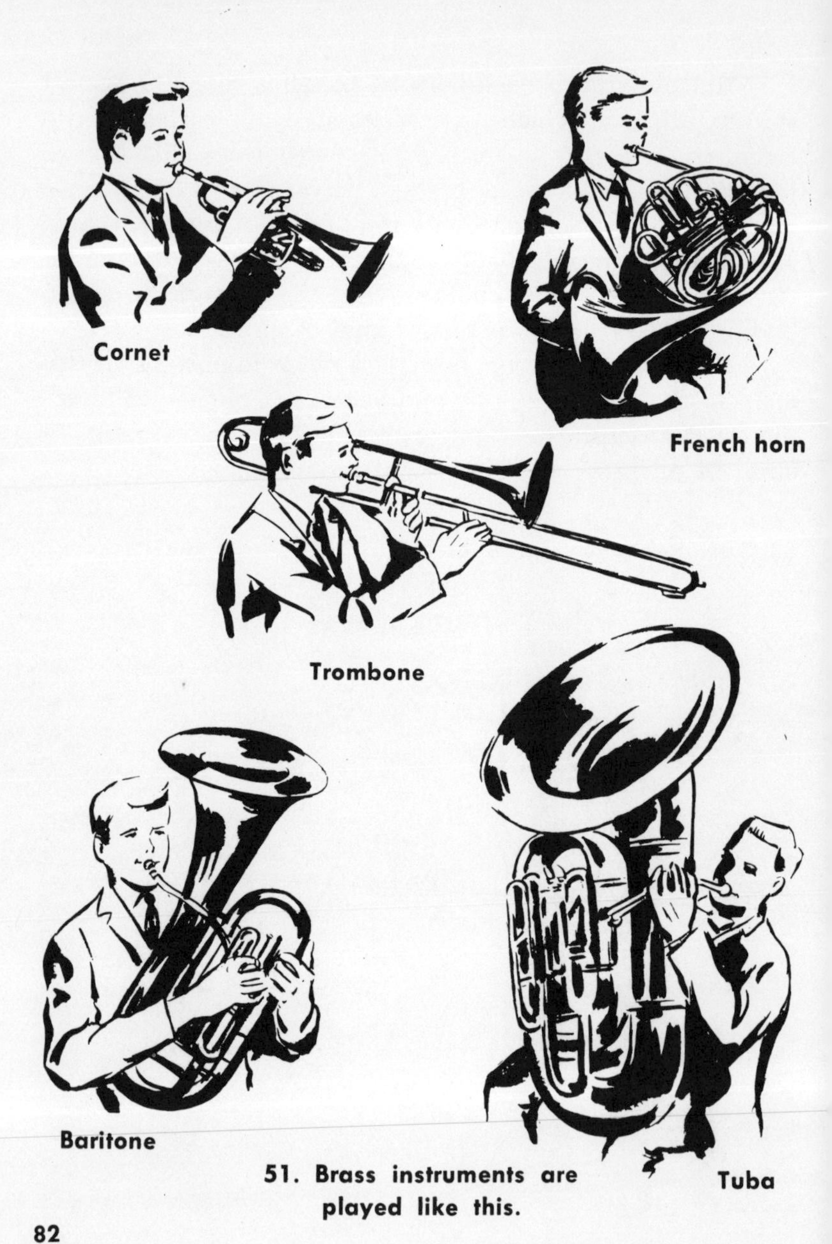

51. Brass instruments are played like this.

The symphony orchestra uses at least four French horns. In the past few years some of the larger jazz groups have begun to use the horn for special effects.

An instrument called the *mellophone* looks like the French horn but has a different sound and is less complicated to play. It uses the more common piston valve. Mellophones are often included in the school orchestra and band.

SUGGESTED RECORDINGS

Prokofiev: *Peter and the Wolf* (Wolf)
Mendelssohn: *A Midsummer Night's Dream* (Nocturne)
Suppé: *Light Cavalry Overture*
Strauss: *Till Eulenspiegel*
Tschaikowsky: *Symphony No. 5* (Second Movement)
Wagner: *Prelude to Lohengrin*

Trombone

If you could turn back the clock to see an orchestra as it appeared over 400 years ago, you would recognize one instrument easily. The trombone's shape—cylindrical tubing, flaring bell and free-moving slide—has changed very little over the years.

The trombone is interesting because you use a slide to play. The slide is a U-shaped tube that fits snugly over the main tubing, as shown in Illus 52. As you push the slide away from you, the instrument lengthens, the air travels a longer distance, and lower notes are produced. You use your right hand to operate the slide while your left hand holds and balances the instrument. Because of the moving slide, the trombonist requires the most room to play his instrument. If you play the trombone, you'll find yourself in the front row of the marching band!

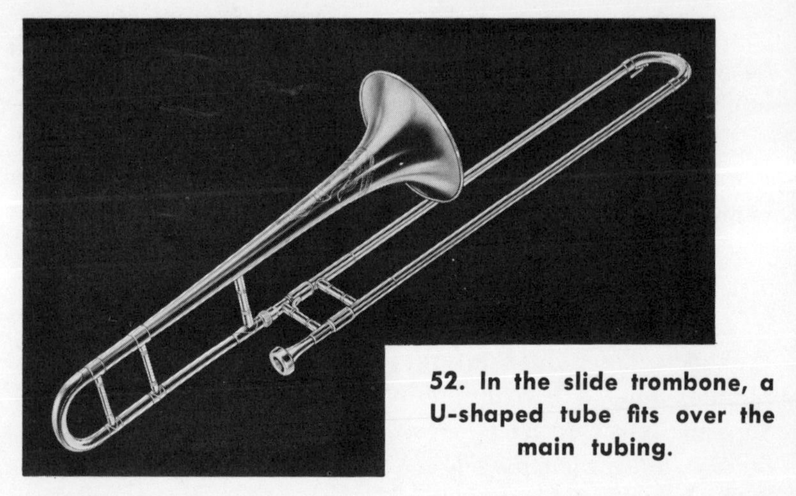

52. In the slide trombone, a U-shaped tube fits over the main tubing.

There are seven playing positions on the slide and at each position, you can play a different series of notes. These seven positions are equivalent to the seven valve combinations of a valve instrument. There is a valve trombone but it's not used often.

The slide on your trombone must have absolute freedom of movement or you won't be able to play notes rapidly and accurately. You must be especially careful not to drop or knock a trombone. The slightest bend or dent will prevent

53. The valve trombone is less frequently played.

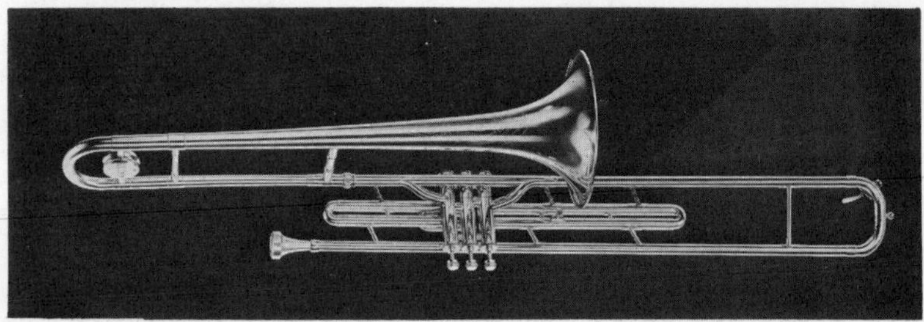

you from moving the slide properly. The slide has to be lubricated with a special light oil, and as soon as it becomes sluggish, you must clean it and apply fresh lubricant.

The most common trombone today is the B-flat tenor. The bass trombone is also frequently used. Symphony orchestras use at least three trombones, two tenors and one bass. Trombones are also important in the concert band and the dance band.

Suggested Recordings

B-flat Tenor Trombone:

Grofé: *Grand Canyon Suite* (On the Trail)
Rimsky-Korsakov: *Scheherazade* (Second Movement)
Tschaikowsky: *Marche Slave* and *1812 Overture*
Wagner: *Lohengrin*—Prelude to Act III

Bass Trombone:

Sibelius: *Finlandia*
Tschaikowsky: *Symphony No. 6* (First Movement)

Tuba

Serpent, helicon, ophicleides, saxhorn, saxtromba—these are some of the odd-sounding names of instruments that preceded our modern low-pitched brasses. Coiled or upright; small, medium or large; bells facing upward, forward or back over the shoulder; held in the arms or placed over the shoulder—out of all this assortment emerged the tuba and its related instruments.

One thing remains the same, and that is the variety of tubas. Today there are many different-sized tubas used in the orchestra and band. The symphony orchestra tuba is

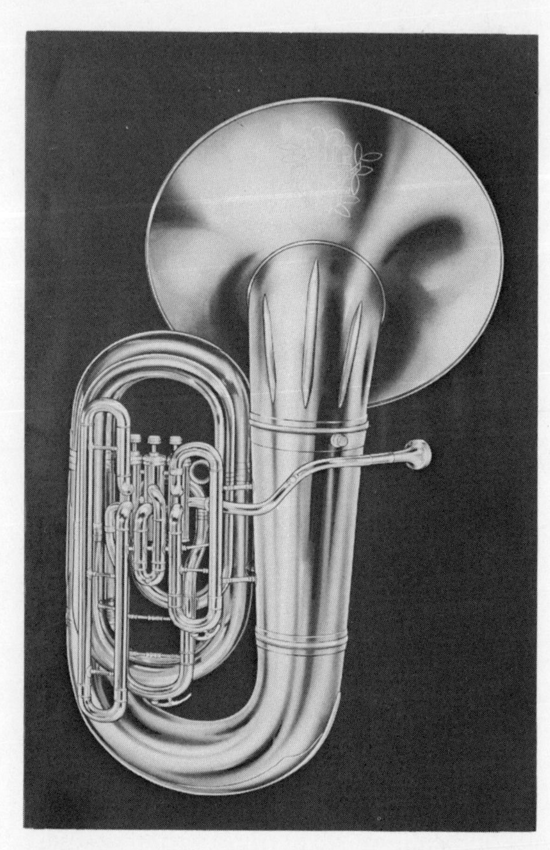

54. Tubas come in many sizes, all fairly large.

generally a C tuba while the band tuba is either an E-flat or double B-flat tuba. The largest tuba has as much as 35 feet of tubing!

Since these instruments are very similar, if you learn to play the tuba well, you will be able to play any of them.

Because instruments in the tuba family are large, they are usually played by large people. But smaller people can and do play them. Proper breathing and posture are more important than size, strength or great wind capacity.

The sousaphone—named after John Philip Sousa, the band director and composer of marches—is the largest instrument in the concert band and the marching band. It is a tuba coiled in such a way that it rests on the player's shoulder. Originally, the huge bell of the sousaphone faced upward, but today it thrusts forward.

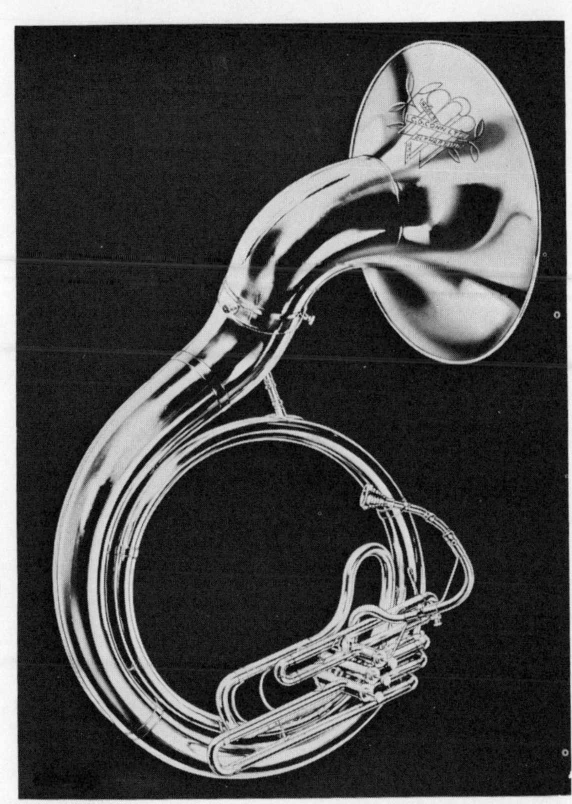

55. The sousaphone, popular in the marching band, is carried over the player's shoulder.

The baritone horn and euphonium look like small tubas and are used primarily in the concert band and marching band. They resemble the trombone in sound. The eupho-

56. The baritone horn looks like a small tuba and sounds something like a trombone.

nium has a larger bore than the baritone horn. This allows for a more mellow sound, and so it is used frequently in the band as a solo instrument. An interesting type of euphonium is the one with two bells, each with separate tubing and an extra valve which, when pressed, opens the smaller bell. This is used for special effects.

You may wonder why there are so many instruments that are so similar. Why can't they all be combined? There's a good reason for the variety and number—each one is different enough in tone quality or range of notes, or both, to justify its separate existence. Perhaps in the years to come we will see an instrument that combines the best features of each. At present, this seems unlikely, but we have seen so many changes made, who knows about the future?

Suggested Recordings

Kleinsinger: *Tubby the Tuba*
Ravel: *Mother Goose Suite* (Beauty and the Beast)
Wagner: *Siegfried's Rhine Journey*

Suggested Recordings of Entire Brass Family

Mussorgsky: *Love Music from Boris Godunov*
Tschaikowsky: *Symphony No. 4* (First Movement)
Wagner: *Ride of the Valkyries*

6. THE PERCUSSION

Who can resist the stirring sound of "a roll of the drums?" And who can resist the drums themselves? The very sight of them makes most of us itch to beat out a strong and rollicking rhythm.

Of course drums are not the only percussion instruments. Any instrument that you play by striking is called a percussion instrument whether you use sticks, beaters, mallets, your hand, or simply strike two objects together. When you strike a percussion instrument the vibration produces sound, but in many cases the sound has no definite pitch or tone. They are primarily rhythm instruments to keep time. Percussion instruments which have no definite pitch are snare drums, bass drum, cymbals, tambourine, gong, triangle and castanets. They are used for special effects as well as for rhythm.

The other instruments in the percussion family play both melody and rhythm. They are called definite-pitch instruments and in this group you find the xylophone, marimba, vibraphone, glockenspiel (bells), chimes, and celeste. The timpani or kettledrums belong here too because you can tune them to different pitches according to the music.

The drummer in a dance band ordinarily plays a bass drum, snare drum, tom-tom, single cymbal on a holder, high-hat (two cymbals on a stand) and accessories. In a marching band and drum corps, the number of drummers varies with the group. In a concert band, there is one snare drum, one bass drum, the timpani and any other instı music might call for—bells, triangle, cymbal, etc usually handled by two or three percussionists, s the instruments are played at the same time.

The percussionist should be acquainted with a number of other less frequently used accessories, such as the wood-block, anvil, cowbell, maracas and bird-whistle. He's the sound-effects man in addition to performing his main function of providing the necessary rhythm, melody and harmony. An accomplished orchestral percussionist can play all of the many instruments described in this chapter. The reason he's able to do this is that there is a great deal of similarity among the various instruments.

57. These are timpani or kettledrums, large copper bowls topped with calfskins.

mpani

Timpani are called kettledrums sometimes because they look somewhat like old-fashioned kettles. Originally they were drums made from clay pots. In the Middle Ages the nobility considered timpani playing their special privilege, and only royalty could own the instruments.

A fascinating drum used in India in the 16th century was called a master drum. Mounted atop an elephant, this silver drum measured 5 feet in diameter and weighed 450 pounds! The player sat on the rim and played it with a silver stick.

In Europe, too, mounted timpani—not on elephants but on horses—were used for military purposes such as marching armies to war. As the timpani were made larger and larger, they were dropped out of military use and the smaller snare and bass drums replaced them. It was approximately 1650 when the timpani were first used with an orchestra. Since that time, they have become very important members of the orchestra and concert band.

The timpani look like oversize copper bowls. Calfskins are stretched across the tops, called the head, and held in place by large metal rims. Screws which pass through these rims allow the skins to be tightened to play a high pitch, or loosened to play a low pitch. Timpani appear in different sizes and in sets, each one tuned to a different pitch. Symphony orchestras use a set of at least three, sometimes four and more.

You play the timpani by striking the skin with timpani sticks, the striking ends of which are balls of felt. You can use either hard or soft balls, depending on the different effects you want to create. To produce a long or continuous sound—called a single-stroke roll—you must rapidly strike the head with first one stick and then the other. You only need one of the timpani to play a roll.

Modern timpani have foot pedals which, when pressed, loosen or tighten the head, like the screws. The pedals enable a player to make rapid changes of pitch which are often necessary in orchestral and band music. The next time you go to a concert, notice how the timpani player leans over his instrument to tune it, one ear close to the skinhead. With one foot on the pedal, he taps the skin lightly and adjusts the pedal to the approximate pitch that he wants. He then uses the hand screws to make fine adjustments and get the exact pitch.

Suggested Recordings

Elgar: *Enigma Variations*
Prokofiev: *Peter and the Wolf* (Hunter's Guns)
Tschaikowsky: *Romeo and Juliet Overture*
Wagner: *Siegfried's Funeral March*

Xylophone

The xylophone has its origin in primitive cultures, especially in Africa, where players struck wooden bars or sticks placed across their legs. The wooden bars of the modern xylophone are mounted on a frame with legs to support it at table height. There are two rows of bars arranged like the white and black keys on the piano keyboard. Underneath each bar is a hollow metal tube called a resonator to increase the sound.

You play the xylophone standing up, striking the bars with mallets held in both hands. The action is fast and energetic and lots of fun. The long bars at the lower or left end of the keyboard produce the low sounds and the bars gradu-

58. Two rows of wooden bars on the xylophone are rapidly struck with mallets.

ally shorten as the pitch goes higher. You play a long note or roll by rapid single strokes, as with the timpani. A xylophone makes beautiful music, alone or in a band or orchestra.

Very closely related to the xylophone are the marimba and vibraphone. The marimba's bars are also made of wood but the resonators are larger than the xylophone's. The vibraphone has steel bars and uses electricity to make the sound louder and also to create a vibrato (shaking) tone. You can play with two, three or four mallets on the marimba and vibraphone, holding one or more with each hand.

SUGGESTED RECORDINGS

Gershwin: *Piano Concerto in F* (Last Movement)
Saint-Saëns: *Danse Macabre*
Saint-Saëns: *Carnival of the Animals* (Fossils)
Shostakovich: *Polka from the Age of Gold Ballet*

Glockenspiel and Bell-Lyra

The glockenspiel consists of steel bars of different sizes arranged like the keys of the piano in a U-shaped frame. You support the instrument with your left hand and play by striking the bars with a mallet held in your right hand.

The bell-lyra, sometimes called orchestra bells, is essen-

Timpani

Xylophone

Marimba

Chimes

Glockenspiel

59. The percussion section provides rhythm.

tially the same instrument. You play it with both hands, a mallet in each.

Both the glockenspiel and bell-lyra have penetrating tones. In parades you hear the sound of the glockenspiel long before you hear the rest of the band!

SUGGESTED RECORDING

Nevin: *A Day in Venice*

Celeste

The celeste is an instrument that resembles a small piano. It is a keyboard instrument with hammers which strike steel bars. Underneath are resonators to increase the sound. The celeste tone is light, graceful and clear.

SUGGESTED RECORDINGS

Grofé: *Grand Canyon Suite* (On the Trail)
Ravel: *Mother Goose Suite* (Empress of the Pagodas)
Tschaikowsky: *The Nutcracker Suite* (Sugar Plum Fairy)

Chimes

The chimes are metal tubes arranged like a keyboard but suspended from a metal frame. There are about 18 in a set, all of different lengths. The long tubes sound low notes and the shorter tubes, the higher notes. You play the chimes with a wooden or rawhide-tipped mallet. They sound very much like melodious church bells.

This is one percussion instrument which doesn't require speed and energy. Each time you strike a note it vibrates and rings for a while before the sound dies out. Therefore you must strike the chimes slowly and separately or you will get a jumbled sound.

Suggested Recordings

Mussorgsky: *A Night on Bald Mountain*
Tschaikowsky: *1812 Overture*

INDEFINITE PITCH PERCUSSION

Bass Drum

The bass drum is an impressive instrument which varies in size from 20 inches to over 40 inches in diameter. Naturally, the larger the size, the louder and deeper is the sound. The shell of the drum is made of wood with skins attached to both sides by metal rods. You can adjust the rods to tighten or loosen the skins.

You play the bass drum with a beater which has a large ball of felt or wool on the striking end and usually a smaller ball on the other end. You can play a roll on the bass drum with two timpani sticks or you can use the regular double-ball beater. You hold the beater with a firm grip at the end with the small ball and rotate your wrist rapidly, striking the head first with the large ball and then with the small ball.

An orchestra, concert band or marching band ordinarily uses one bass drum, and of course the drum beats the rhythm in every dance band.

Suggested Recording

Grieg: *Peer Gynt Suite* (Arabian Dance)

Snare Drum (Side Drum), Tenor Drum and Tom-Tom

Like the bass drum, the snare or side drum consists of a wooden or metal shell (14 or 15 inches in diameter)

60. A drum ensemble for a dance band consists of bass drum, tom-tom, snare drum, cymbal and high-hat. Accessories include wooden block and cowbell.

with skins on either side. To tighten or loosen the skin you use a drum key on the metal rods. Look at the bottom of the snare drum. You will see lengths of catgut or wires (called snares) stretched across the bottom skin. These snares vibrate each time you strike the top or batter head with drumsticks.

Before you can play the drums you must learn to hold the sticks properly. Look at Illus. 61 and 62 carefully and you will see that each stick is held differently.

Usually, beginning drum students play on a p
drum pad which is available at most music stores.
drum practicing can be annoying to other members of your family and your neighbors, we recommend that you use these pads – if you want to be permitted to continue playing the drum. You can even make your own pad:

(1) Select a piece of wood (¾-inch thick plywood is best) approximately 8 inches square. (2) Then cut out a piece of thick hard rubber (an old discarded tire or a rubber tile might do) to fit the square, either the same size or smaller as it need not cover the entire surface. (3) Nail or cement this rubber piece onto the wooden surface. This is your playing surface. (4) On the other side of the now padded wooden square, nail or cement a strip of wood (any kind) across one end. This allows the drum pad to rest on an angle – the raised end on your left when you play. (See Illus. 63.)

Drumsticks cost only about 50 cents to $1.00 but you

61. You hold sticks and wire brushes in the same way.

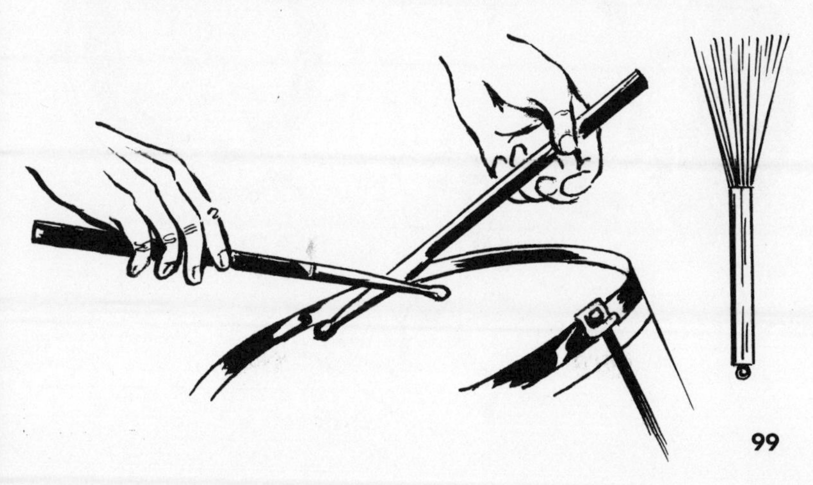

62.

have to make certain that they're not warped before you buy them. To test for warping, roll the sticks on any flat surface. If the sticks roll evenly, they are good.

In the dance band, the drum player uses wire brushes as well as sticks on the snare drum. The wires on these brushes are arranged in a fan shape and attached to a handle.

The snare drum plays an important part in almost all musical groups: the orchestra, concert band, marching band, dance band, drum corps and bugle corps.

The tenor drum is a large snare drum played mostly in marching bands. The tom-tom, similar to a snare drum, has no snares. You'll find the tom-tom primarily in dance bands.

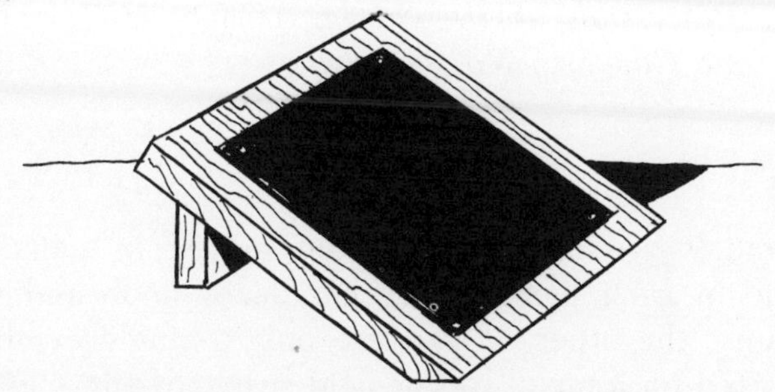

63. A drum pad is useful for practicing.

Suggested Recordings

Snare or Side Drum:

Bizet: *Carmen Suite* (Les Dragons d'Alcala)
Rimsky-Korsakov: *Capriccio Espagnol*

Tenor Drum:

Ravel: *Bolero*

Triangle

As the name implies, the triangle is a solid steel bar bent into the shape of a triangle which you strike with a small steel rod. It has a penetrating sound with no definite pitch. The triangle must vibrate freely in order to produce the proper sound, so you must suspend it by a cord or string. To play a roll, you hold the beater inside the triangle and rapidly beat against two sides, close to a corner.

Suggested Recordings

Grieg: *Peer Gynt Suite* (Anitra's Dance)
Ivanow: *Procession of the Sardar* (Caucasian Sketches)
Liszt: *Piano Concerto No. 1 in E-flat*

Cymbals

Cymbals are brass discs often played in pairs. You hold one in each hand by its handle or knob and strike one against the other. If you use only a single cymbal, it is supported on a metal rod or held suspended in one hand and you strike it with snare drumsticks, brushes or a beater – whichever creates the sound effect you want. The bass drum player in a band has one cymbal attached to the top of his drum and holds the other one in his left hand. In this way, he can play the cymbals and beat the drum at the same time.

The drummer in a dance band uses a device called a high-hat, two cymbals on a stand. With a foot pedal, he operates the top cymbal which moves lightly up and down, coming in contact with the lower stationary cymbal.

Suggested Recordings

Grieg: *Peer Gynt Suite* (Arabian Dance)
Respighi: *The Fountains of Rome*
Tschaikowsky: *Marche Slave*

Tam-Tam or Chinese Gong

You may know the tam-tam by its more familiar name of the Chinese gong. It is an ancient Chinese instrument made of brass or bronze hung in a frame. Suspended like this, it vibrates freely when struck with a large drum beater.

Suggested Recording

Balakirev: *Tone Poem, "Russia"*

Castanets

Castanets are pieces of hard wood shaped like spoons without handles. You use them in pairs, striking them together in the palm of the hand. Some castanets are attached to a handle which you shake to play.

Suggested Recordings

Bizet: *Carmen Suite* (Entr'acte)
Tschaikowsky: *1812 Overture*

Suggested Recordings of Entire Percussion Family

Chavez: *Toccata for Percussion*
Haydn: *Toy Symphony*

7. OTHER INSTRUMENTS

Accordion

Some of our most popular musical instruments are not used in orchestras and concert bands. The accordion is used primarily as a solo instrument and often it accompanies group singing and folk music. It's often used as a substitute for the piano and that is one of the reasons for its increasing popularity today. People have found they can easily carry this portable instrument to places where a piano is not available.

The accordion is a full-bodied, melodious instrument. Like the piano, it produces both melody and harmony. It is an important member of many dance bands and some school orchestras even use accordions but this is not common. In the last few years, many accordion bands, made up of only accordion players, have been formed.

The accordion consists of pleated bellows, a keyboard on one side similar to the one on a piano and buttons on the other side. As you move the pleated bellows back and forth with your left hand you force air against metal reeds which are located inside the accordion. The forced air sets the reeds in motion and produces musical sounds.

There are two sets of reeds in the accordion. One set vibrates when you pull the bellows apart and the other set vibrates when you push them together. This action enables you to play any notes regardless of the direction

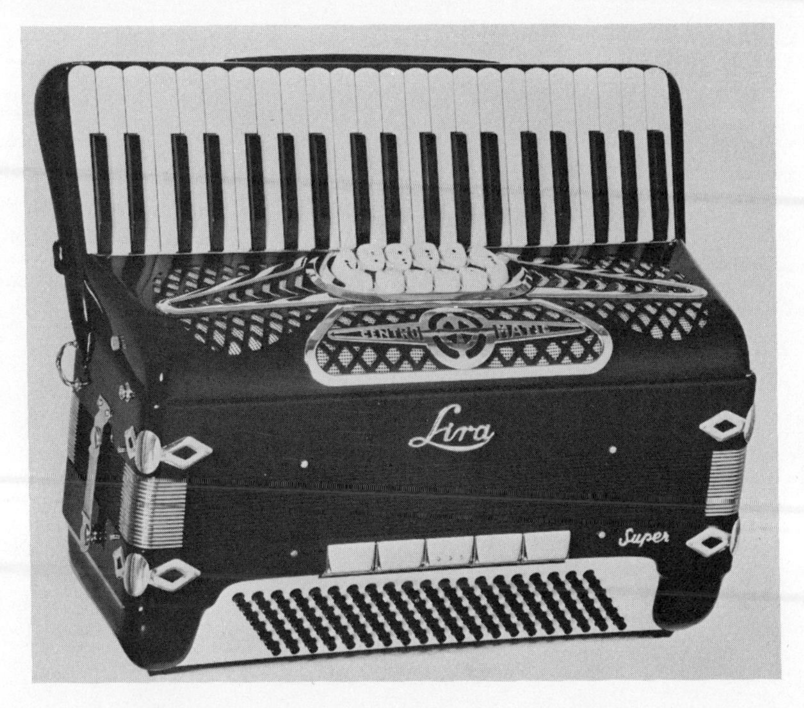

64. The 120 bass accordion is named for the number of buttons it has.

in which the bellows are moving. Your left hand, in addition to moving the bellows together and apart, also fingers the buttons, which play the low notes or chords (several notes at once).

You can play the accordion either softly or loudly. To increase the sound, some accordionists attach a small microphone to the accordion and the amplifier connected to the microphone permits the accordion to be heard in very large halls and auditoriums.

Accordions are named for the number of buttons that

they have in the bass. For example, the smallest one with 12 buttons is a 12 bass accordion, and one with 210 buttons, the largest, is called 210 bass. The most popular accordion is the 120 bass which comes in different sizes but always has 120 buttons (40 bass or low notes and 80 chords). Small children can start on the small 12 bass or small 120 bass accordion.

Your right hand fingers the keyboard and usually plays the melody while your left hand plays the harmony (chords). Most accordions also have switches above the keyboard which are marked clarinet, violin, bassoon, piccolo, etc., and when you press a switch, the accordion sounds like an imitation of that instrument. These switches also enable you to play very low or very high notes.

If you want to play the accordion well, you must learn to move the bellows back and forth smoothly—that is, when you change the direction of the bellows, there should not be a noticeable stop; otherwise the sound would be interrupted.

Recorder

The recorder was replaced by the flute during the Middle Ages but it has become once again a popular instrument.

Little change has been made on the recorder since its use in the Middle Ages. It is still a simply constructed instrument with holes but no keys. Recorders are available in soprano and tenor (C recorder) sizes, as well as alto and bass (F recorders).

To play the recorder, you blow into the opening on the top (mouthpiece). Then you use all the fingers on your right hand, including the thumb, to finger the top

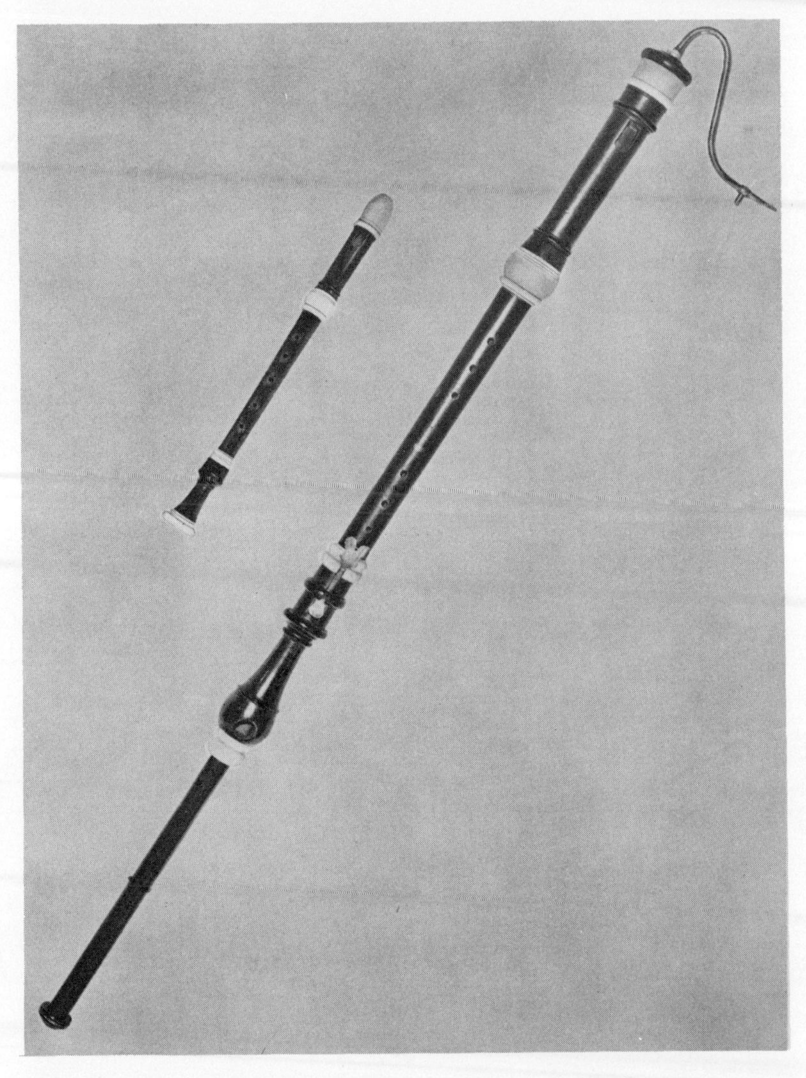

65. The alto and bass recorder, made in the 17th century, are now museum pieces. Recorders have become popular again today.

holes, and the fingers on your left hand to cover the four bottom holes.

The following are a few of the fingerings for the soprano recorder in C:

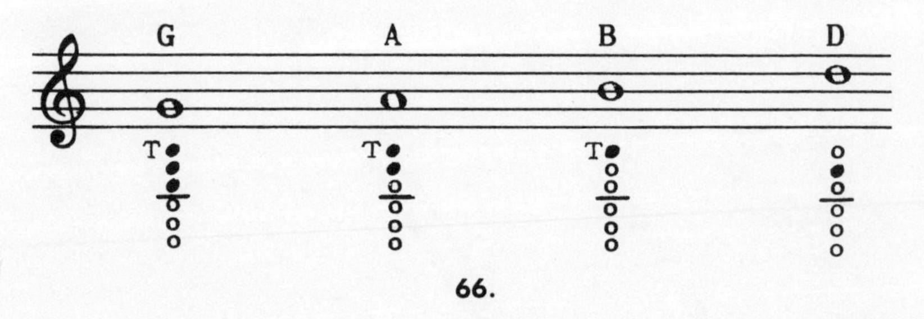

66.

The filled-in circles represent fingers which you must place on holes. (The T is for the thumb.)

By learning the fingerings to the above four notes, you can try this melody:

67.

You can see that the recorder is fairly easy to play. Of course there will be many other notes and fingerings to learn if you want to play more difficult melodies. The recorder is not a band or orchestral instrument but is played alone or in recorder groups.

Harmonica

Many people consider the harmonica a musical toy, but in the hands of an artist it becomes a true instrument. It's a fine instrument to learn to play – you can carry it in your pocket wherever you go and produce it at a moment's notice to entertain friends or to keep yourself company, indoors or out, walking or riding.

The harmonica has metal reeds which are set into vibration when you blow or inhale through the top openings. By blowing through a hole you produce one pitch; by inhaling or drawing on the same hole, you get a com-

68. The harmonica, when played well, is far more than a toy.

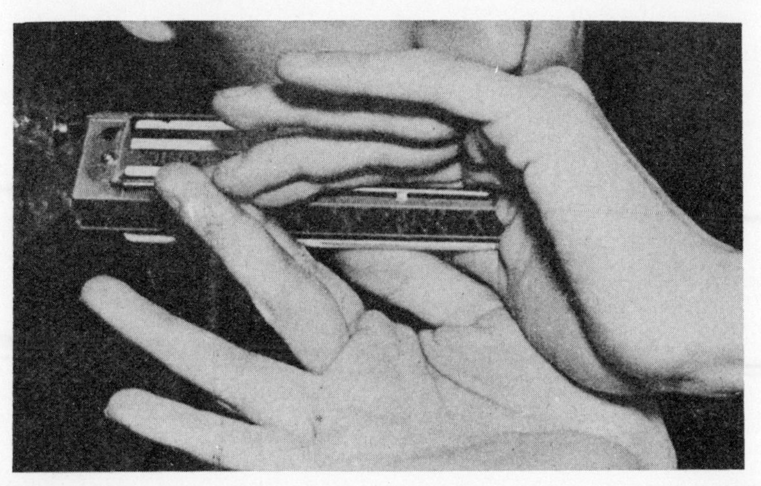

pletely different pitch. This is because each hole has two reeds — one vibrates when you blow into it and the other vibrates when you exhale.

The three major types of harmonicas are the single-hole, the double-hole, and the chromatic. It's best to start on the single-hole which has ten single holes, is the least expensive of the three and the least complicated. If the ten-hole harmonica is a C harmonica, blowing into the fourth hole gives you the note C; if it is a D harmonica, blowing into the fourth hole gives you the note D.

Before you start to play, make certain that you hold the harmonica so that the lower notes are to the left and the higher notes to the right. In order to play properly, you close your lips but leave a small opening over the hole or holes to be played. Hold the harmonica with both hands and blow into a hole. Now inhale. Notice the difference in pitch?

Using the G harmonica, let's try playing a few simple tunes requiring only the holes 4, 5 and 6. Blow into the fourth hole first to locate the note G. When you inhale on the fourth hole, you get the note A. Now blow into holes 4, 5 and 6, and they'll give you the notes G, B and D; when

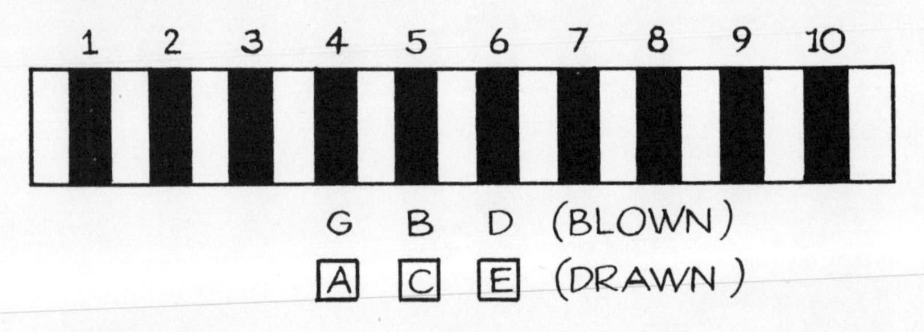

69.

you draw on these holes, you'll get A, C and E. (See Illus. 69.)

Now by following the illustration and practicing, you should be able to play *Jingle Bells* and *Twinkle, Twinkle Little Star*.

Jingle Bells

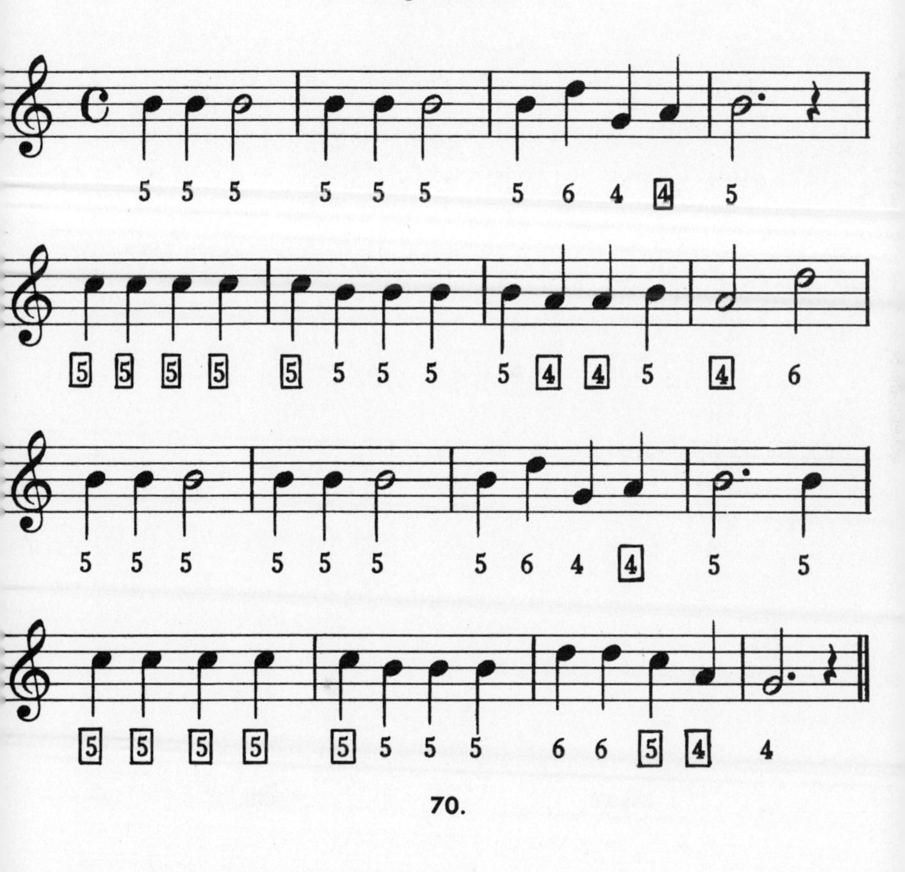

70.

Twinkle, Twinkle Little Star

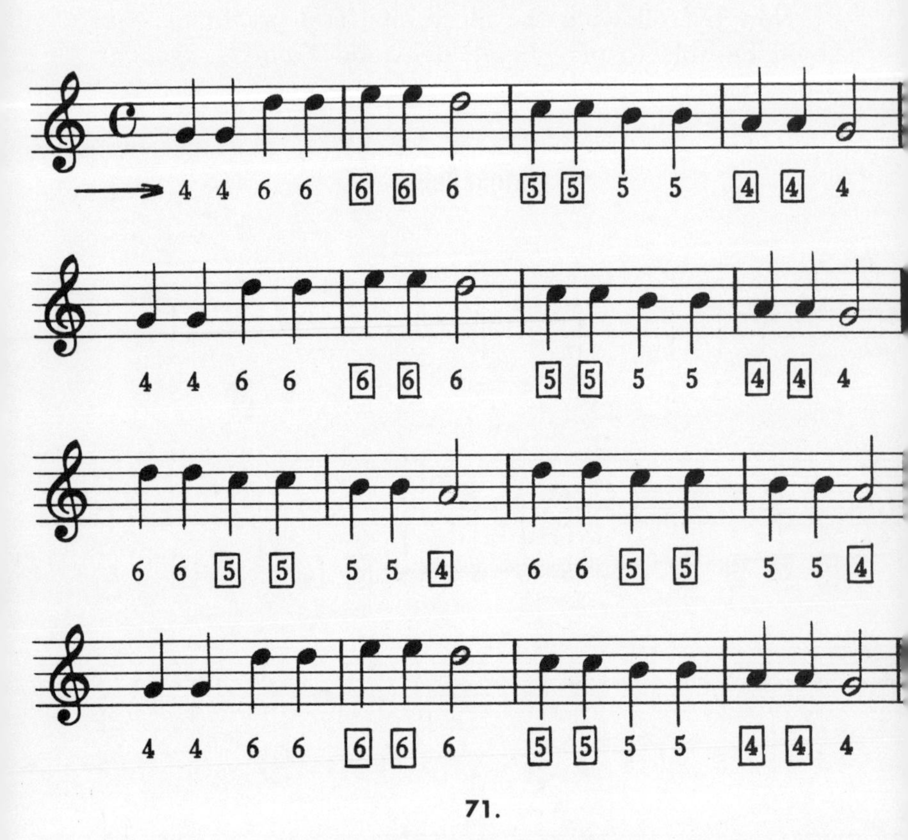

71.

Ukelele

The ukelele is an instrument resembling a small guitar. It is made of either plastic or wood and has four strings and a fretted fingerboard. You play the ukelele sitting or standing, holding it against your body. Using four fingers of your left hand (the thumb is not used) for fingering, your right hand strums the strings with the fingers or with a pick. It came to the United States mainland from Hawaii.

Most ukelele music gives you finger directions. These are diagrams showing the four strings and frets, with a black circle indicating where to place your fingers. Where there is no black circle, you play only the open strings. If more than one finger is needed for a chord, more than one black circle will be shown.

Here is an example of a fingering diagram for the background chords for *Row, Row, Row Your Boat*.

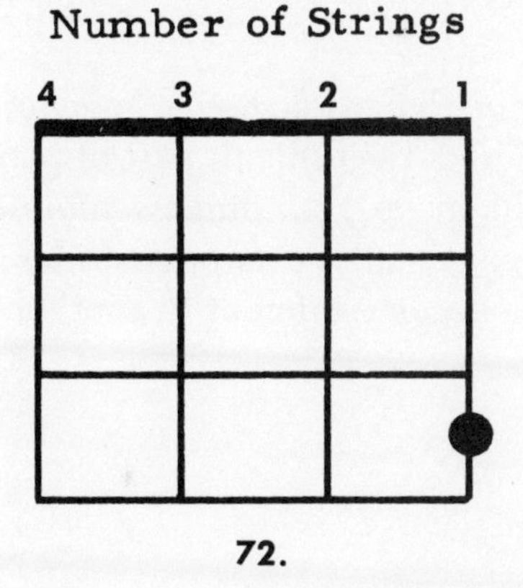

Place your first (index) finger of the left hand on the first string between the frets shown in the diagram. Now strum on all the strings and sing the melody to *Row Your Boat*. The ukelele, as you can see, is mainly an accompaniment instrument.

The chord you just played is one of the simplest. Now try to play this chord:

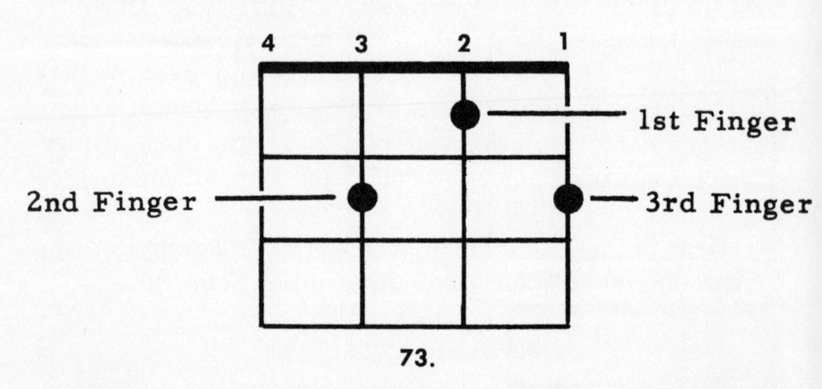

73.

Make certain that each finger touches only the string marked for it. This is the difficult part of playing the ukelele, but practice will make your fingers nimble.

Now, using the above two positions of two chords, you can play the accompaniment to another melody, *Merrily We Roll Along*.

Merrily We Roll Along

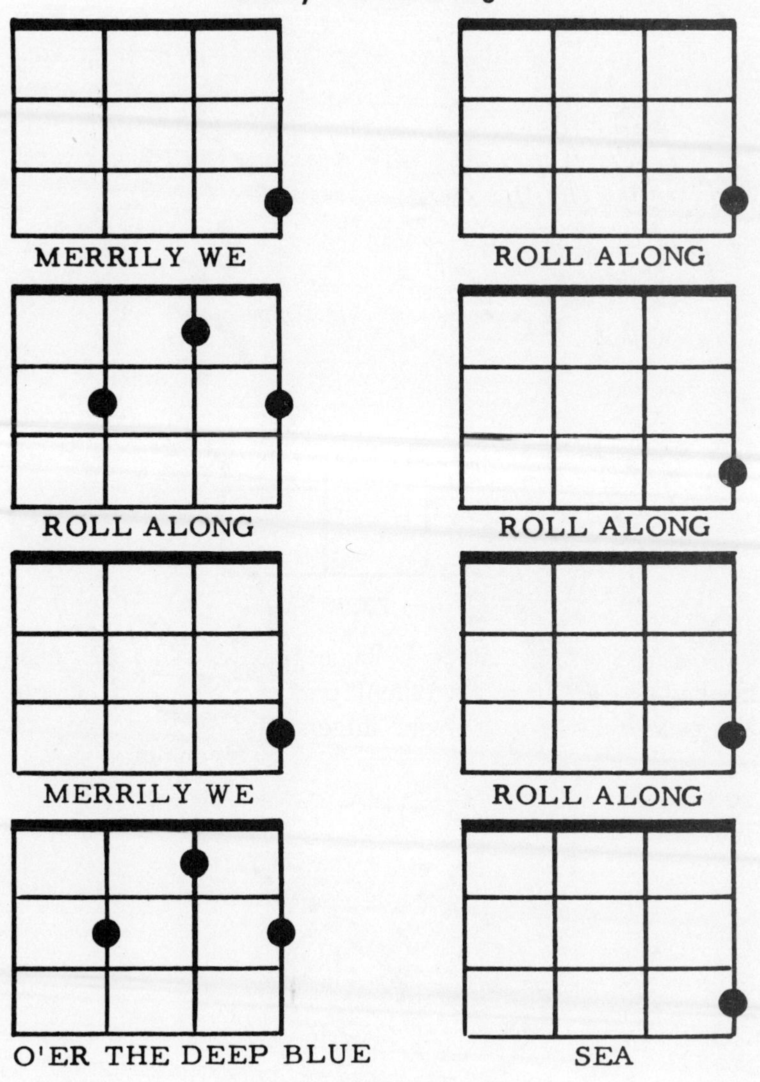

74.

75.

Banjo

Banjo

In the early 30's, the plunk-plunk of a banjo was a common sound, but gradually it was replaced by the guitar. The banjo has a long neck and a tambourine-like body. The number of strings varies from four to nine depending on the size of the instrument. You strum the banjo with a pick or plectrum. It's used primarily to accompany singing. At one time banjos were widely used in jazz bands, but you seldom hear any today. Occasionally, the banjo is still used as a solo instrument.

Mandolin

The mandolin is a pear-shaped instrument related to the guitar. Its eight strings are tuned the same way as violin strings, but there are two strings to each pitch. The mandolin, which originated in Spain, came to America around 1880 and became quite popular. Today there are mandolin clubs and societies in most large cities. You play the mandolin by rapidly strumming the strings with a plectrum. School music groups don't use the mandolin.

Zither

It's only in recent years that the zither became a familiar instrument. The haunting music of the theme from the movie "The Third Man" brought the zither new popularity, yet this ancient string instrument was played as far back as the 8th century B.C.

We see several types of zithers today, but the most common one is the board zither which is simply a sound box strung with 30 or 40 strings. To play the zither, you pluck the strings with your fingers or with a plectrum. It's usually heard in connection with folk music.

76. The zither, an ancient instrument, often accompanies folk singing today.

8. THE VOICE

Singing is one of the oldest forms of music, and the human voice is often considered the most beautiful and most sensitive of all musical instruments. Certainly it's one of the most flexible. Think of the many things you can do with your voice – whisper, speak softly, shout, hum, sing and imitate many sounds! You can do all these things without any special training or practice.

Long before you were able to talk, you were producing musical sounds. As a baby, your first toys were likely to be musical toys. You listened and responded when your mother sang to you, and before long, you were imitating those sounds. As you grew older, you began to sing your own songs – nursery songs and even made-up songs. You sang while you played your favorite games. During your earliest years in school, you learned many more songs. Singing is a natural, enjoyable activity which can bring you pleasure all your life.

Most schools give you early vocal training and also teach sight singing to prepare you for group singing in choruses, glee clubs and choirs. Group participation is a fine experience for everyone and particularly valuable if you plan to study the voice.

You were born with this instrument, but how does it work? In the back of the mouth you have an organ called the larynx. Across this larynx extend two membranes (thin tissues) which we call our vocal cords. When you want to make a sound, you take a breath and fill up your lungs with air which then travels up the windpipe and passes through an opening between the vocal cords. The amount of air controls your tone. The more air you use, the louder you sound. This opening, called the glottis, controls the pitch of your voice. When the opening is large, the glottis relaxes and your pitch is low. When the opening is small, the glottis becomes tense and your pitch is high. That is why your voice often gets squeaky when you are angry or excited and your throat "closes up."

The length of the vocal cords also helps in determining pitch. The vocal cords and larynx of a young boy are about the same size as those of a young girl, and that's why there is little difference in pitch between a boy's and girl's voice. As a boy grows to adolescence, his larynx and vocal cords also grow – especially the larynx. The Adam's apple, which is part of the larynx, enlarges and becomes more noticeable. This growth causes his voice to become low-pitched and he gradually develops a man's voice. A girl's voice also changes, but there is so little growth in her larynx and vocal cords that the change in her voice is not as apparent. Her voice does develop, however, from a childlike sound to a full rich mature one.

Proper breathing is a "must" for good singing. You have to breathe with the diaphragm, which is a muscle located between the chest and abdomen. Place your hand over your abdomen, below the ribs, and feel it move as you breathe. Before you start to sing, you fill your lungs with air and expand your diaphragm. As you sing, the air controlled by the diaphragm travels up the windpipe, through the glottis, and out the mouth. This correct breathing helps you to produce good tone. When you hear a good singer, actor or speaker, you may be sure he is using his diaphragm.

77. Your breathing is very important when you sing. Fill your lungs with air and expand your diaphragm.

When you sing a tone correctly, the air in your mouth and nose vibrates, and the roof of the mouth acts as a sounding board.

Maybe you think you can't sing, or that you're a "monotone." A so-called "monotone" is someone who has difficulty distinguishing pitch, but anyone who can talk can learn to sing.

If you think you can't sing, perhaps your difficulty can be traced to the lack of singing around you during your early years. Perhaps when you entered grade school your teacher told you to listen and not sing because your singing "spoiled" the class performance. Of course you did not listen either, and simply became bored. By not singing and not listening properly, you became less and less aware of the direction of sound in music – that is, whether the sound moves higher or lower – and of course you have difficulty keeping in tune when you do try. While you are still young, you can overcome this difficulty with time and practice and the help of a teacher or other competent person. Learning to play an instrument sometimes proves helpful too.

Singing is always a popular pastime. Most schools and communities have choruses or other types of vocal groups. Take advantage of them. You will find the experience enjoyable, stimulating and rewarding. If you wish to study voice seriously, these groups offer valuable experience in solo and group singing.

Anyone can sing and everyone should sing for the sheer fun of it, but to sing correctly and to develop singing into a special art, you need training as with any other instrument.

Now that you have read about the different ways to make music, which instrument is for you? Perhaps when you first started reading this book you had some idea of what you wanted to play. Have you changed your mind? Or are you sticking by your first decision?

Whichever instrument you choose, you have a lifetime of pleasure ahead of you.

INDEX